GREAT CITIES OF THE WORLD PAST AND PRESENT

LONDON

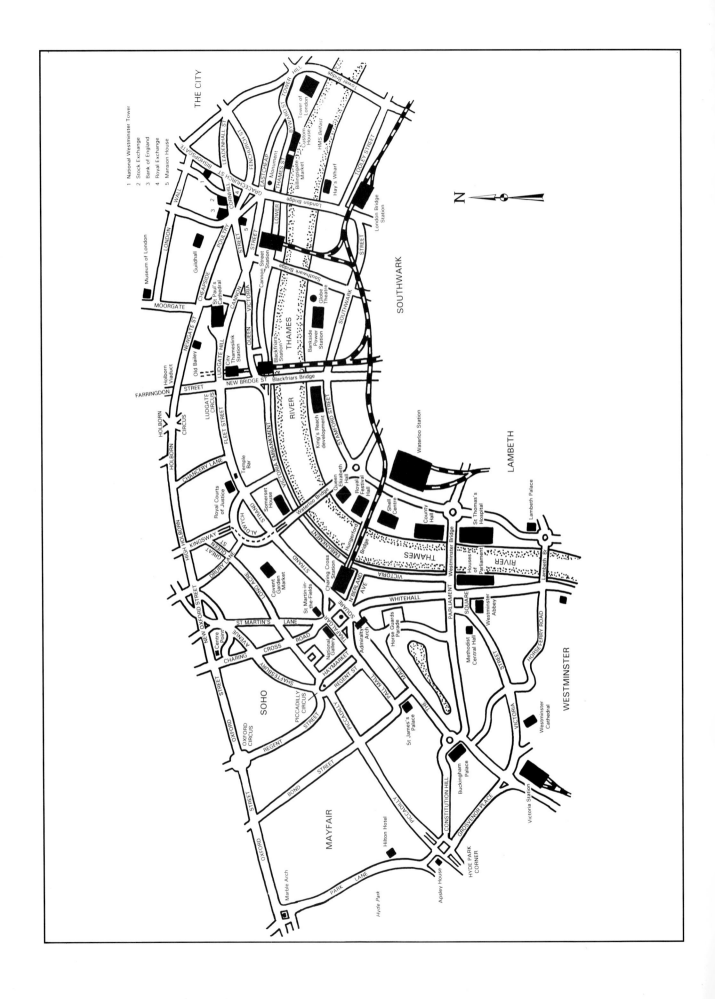

GREAT CITIES OF THE WORLD PAST AND PRESENT

LONDON

A nostalgic look at the capital since 1945

Will & Tricia Adams

Foreword by Lionel Bart

Past & Present Publishing Ltd

First published in June 1997

British Library Cataloguing in Publication Data

A catalogue record for this book is available from the British Library.

ISBN 1 85895 108 9

Past & Present Publishing Ltd
Unit 5
Home Farm Close
Church Street
Wadenhoe
Peterborough PE8 5TE
Tel (01832) 720440
Fax (01832) 720531
e-mail: pete@slinkp-p.demon.co.uk

Printed and bound in Great Britain

ACKNOWLEDGEMENTS

Someone once wrote that if you steal from one author, it's plagiarism; if you steal from many, it's research. Well, a good deal of 'theft' has occurred in the research from this book, and while the principal titles consulted are listed below, we would like in particular to express our gratitude for the scholarship of Ben Weinreb and Christopher Hibbert, Editors of *The London Encyclopaedia* (published by Macmillan). This is without doubt the essential reference book on London, its 1,060 pages crammed with more comprehensive yet readable information on the capital than any other available. Anyone with more than a passing interest in London's history *must* have a copy. The other indispensable handbook that we always carried with us was Nicholas Pevsner and Bridget Cherry's *The Buildings of England: London*, Volumes 1 and 2 (published by Penguin), covering London north and south of the Thames respectively. Again, the essential scholarship is leavened by an acerbic architectural criticism that is pure joy. Don't set off through London on foot without it!

We would also like to express our gratitude to the contributors of the 'past' photographs. We were very fortunate to be able to obtain most of the views from just a few private sources: Neil Davenport and his late father, Arthur Davenport; Frank Hornby and, through him, N. L. Browne and A. J. Pike; and Allan Mott, who allowed us access to the C. F. B. Penley collection and that of his late father, Charles Mott. The other important source was the excellent Photo Library of the London Transport Museum, Covent Garden, and we would like to thank Sheila Taylor and Jane Ramsay for their valued assistance. The other photographers are credited individually, and we are most grateful for their keen interest in and help with this project.

Many other people helped in many ways with the preparation of this book, and we would like to express our thanks to John Broughton, for developing and printing the 'present' views so expertly; Colin Whyman, for arranging access to the top of the Shell Tower to take the required 'present' views, and Shell for granting the facility; John Day at the Department of Transport for furnishing traffic statistics; Natasha at Guinness Archives; Prudential Assurance at Minster Court; Sally Mason and Richard Belcham at the South Bank Centre; and the library staff of Westminster City Archives.

Finally, we would like to thank to Lionel Bart for finding time to contribute such a splendid Foreword.

BIBLIOGRAPHY

Barker, Felix, and Jackson, Peter *London: 2000 years of a city and its people* (Cassell Ltd, 1974)

Cameron, Robert, and Cooke, Alistair *Above London* (The Bodley Head, 1980)

Day, John R. *London's Trams and Trolleybuses* (London Transport, 1977)

Halliwell, Leslie, with Purser, Philip *Halliwell's Television Companion*, 2nd edition (Paladin, 1985)

Hilditch, Neville (compiled by) *In Praise of London* (Frederick Muller Ltd, 1944)

Guide to London, 54th edition (Ward, Lock & Co, c1940)

Jackson, Alan A. *London's Termini* (David & Charles, 1969)

Jackson, Alan A., and Croome, Desmond F. *Rails Through the Clay: a history of London's tube railways* (George Allen & Unwin, 1962)

Jones, Edward, and Woodward, Christopher *A Guide to the Architecture of London* (Weidenfeld & Nicolson, 1983)

Kent, William (edited by) *An Encyclopaedia of London* (J. M. Dent & Sons Ltd, 1937)

Mee, Arthur *The King's England: London*, 6th impression (Hodder & Stoughton, 1951)

Middleditch, Michael *The Penguin London Mapguide* (Penguin Books, 1994)

Nicholson, Louise *London: Louise Nicholson's Definitive Guide* (revised edition, The Bodley head, 1990)

Pevsner, Nikolaus, and Cherry, Bridget *The Buildings of England: London*, Volume 1, 3rd edition (Penguin Books, 1973)

Volume 2 (Penguin Books, 1983)

Reed, John *RT Jubilee: fifty years of a classic London bus* (Silver Link Publishing Ltd, 1989)

Walker, John (edited by) *Halliwell's Filmgoer's Companion*, 10th edition (HarperCollins, 1993)

Halliwell's Film Guide, 8th edition (Grafton, 1992)

Weinreb, Ben, and Hibbert, Christopher (edited by) *The London Encyclopaedia*, revised edition (Macmillan Reference Books, 1995)

CONTENTS

CONVERSION TABLE

When one looks back a few decades at the prices of things, it's easy to think that just because everything cost less then, it was cheaper than it is today - but *in real terms*, of course, many things are in fact *cheaper* now, relative to our disposable income. The accompanying table shows how average wages and the prices of several staple products have changed over the decades. It is of necessity only a rough, 'round figures' guide, but it is interesting to see that while a Mars bar has gone up 10 times and a pint of bitter 20 times, wages have gone up some 36 times! The earlier figures have been converted to the nearest decimal equivalent to make the comparison easier.

	1950	1960	1970	1980	1990
Average weekly wage	£7.29	£14.10	£25.90	£109.50	£263.10
Pint of milk	2p	3p	5p	16½p	32p
Pint of bitter	5p	6p	24p	35½p	£1
Average white loaf	2½p	5p	11p	34p	53p
Mars bar	2p	2½p	3p	14p	21p

£sd/decimal conversion
2½ old pennies (d) = 1 new penny (p)
6d = 2½p
1 shilling (s) = 5p
2s 6d = 12½p
10 shillings = 50p
20 shillings = £1

Thus 22s 6d is the equivalent of £1 2s 6d, or £1 12½p.

These photographs were chosen specifically as a frontispiece to give some idea of the transformation that London, and particularly the City, has undergone since the end of the Second World War. In the **BARBICAN** area some 35 acres were devastated, and the aftermath can be seen in the 'past' picture, dated 24 August 1953. Looking westwards from outside Moorgate station, it gives a good impression of London's post-war bomb-site landscape, with St Paul's still standing sentinel over the devastation, as it did during the 57 consecutive nights that the capital was bombed in 1940-41.

However, it wasn't long before reconstruction was being planned. Initial schemes were drawn up in 1956-59, to provide a residential rather than commercial complex, indicative of the enlightened socialism of the day. Over 2,000 flats were to be built to house 6,500 people, part to be accommodated in three 412-foot towers, then the tallest residential blocks in Europe. The first part was completed in 1966, and the whole Barbican complex was finished at the end of the 1970s. Its rather severe concrete construction and interminable steps and walkways (like trails of breadcrumbs, coloured lines are painted on the paving to prevent people from losing their way) have become so familiar, and somewhat discredited, throughout the country since the 1950s that the effect today is seen as more bleak than bold, despite the trees and lake.

An exact replica of the scene is impossible due to intervening buildings, but believe it or not the second photograph is approximately the same view in 1996, taken a little to the left and a few yards further west. St Paul's is now obscured by the futuristic architecture along London Wall, but the common feature is the tower of 11th-century St Giles Cripplegate (extreme right); it escaped the great Fire of 1666 but was gutted in the Blitz. Restored in 1952-60 as the parish church of the new Barbican development, it is famous for the marriage of Oliver Cromwell in 1620 and as the burial place of the poet John Milton; whether the latter would consider the new Cityscape as Paradise Lost or Paradise Regained is perhaps open to question. . .
Arthur Davenport/WA

FOREWORD

Lionel Bart

I had a house in Malibu, California, for a while, and one day I was walking along the beach when I heard a voice behind me say 'Mile End Road!'. It was the American comic and film director Mel Brooks, who'd spent time in the East End of London as a child. I said, 'How did you know?', and he said 'It's the way you walk.'

I was born in London and have always been a Londoner, and despite having travelled a great deal over the years, there's nowhere in the world like it. I was born in Brick Lane, Whitechapel, and was a kid during the Blitz. The changes that were wrought on London in those days were dramatic and instant - an age-old familiar landmark would be there when you went into the shelter, and would be completely gone when you emerged. One night some of us decided not to go down the shelter but to hide under the stairs, armed with crisps and Tizer. They dug us out after a couple of days! Some 15 years later I wrote a show called *Blitz!*, which was about my childhood in the war. It was on at the Adelphi on the Strand and included an air raid siren; each time it went off on stage people above a certain age passing the theatre in a narrow side street used to flinch and cross to the other pavement.

As kids we used to go 'up West' to central London team-handed. It was five miles from the Mile End Road, and we would walk, because we had no money for bus fares. One day we were walking along the Strand and saw two chaps who looked liked Laurel and Hardy. We started whistling their theme tune, and when they turned round it *was* Laurel and Hardy! They were staying at the Savoy. My friends ran off, but I was transfixed so they walked back to talk to me. They took me to the Black and White milk bar in Charing Cross Road - one of Forte's first. That was how I came to know Stan Laurel.

I then won a scholarship to St Martin's School of Art, and travelled daily to Soho. I lived almost a double life - an East End boy at night and a Soho Johnny during the day! I got jobs painting scenery at the Unity Theatre in Mornington Crescent near King's Cross and getting a feel for the world of entertainment. Everything was beginning to change in the early '50s, and I was lucky to be in at the beginning. It was the era of 'skiffle' - all you needed was a guitar, a tea-chest 'bass' and a washboard (I played the washboard!). The influx of Italians brought with it the new phenomenon of the coffee bar, which inspired one of my early songs, 'Oh, for a cup of tea, instead of a cappuccino'! It was the first of my songs to be broadcast, on the Billy Cotton Band Show, and it was a great thrill to hear it on the air.

Eventually I moved from the East End to a room in

Gloucester Place, near Baker Street - in fact, the room wasn't much bigger than the bed - and I used to walk to Soho from there. In those days I used to compose songs as I walked along, using the paving stones to fix the tempo. That way I could hold the song until I could get somewhere to write it down.

London figured prominently in the first two musicals I was involved in, in 1959. I wrote *Fings Ain't Wot They Used T'Be* about a Soho gangster who returned to the streets after ten years in prison. In the same year I wrote the lyrics for *Lock Up Your Daughters*, the first production mounted by Bernard Miles's Mermaid Theatre, the first new theatre

in London for 300 years. It was only expected to run for a few weeks, but lasted six months, and has recently been revived.

Then in 1960 *Oliver!* had its first performance. Again it was my love of London that led me to Dickens's novel, set around Clerkenwell and the docks where I grew up. In fact, a taxi-driver pointed out to me recently that in the film version, the song 'Consider Yourself' dances its way through the various London markets - Covent Garden, Billingsgate and Spitalfields - in the correct geographical sequence, along the route that people would take towards the East End. I had to admit that the designer and choreographer had to take some of the credit!

Covent Garden is a place that has really changed. Years ago, in my drinking days, Brendan Behan, Richard Harris, Peter O'Toole and I would wind up there for a drink in the morning, and there were the porters with maybe nine baskets of fruit carried on their heads - there was a great atmosphere there. Fleet Street is another place where that air of industrial hubbub has disappeared. I worked in a graphic artists studio there for a few months. It was my first - and last - job working for someone else!

Today places like Covent Garden are given over to what you might call pedestrianised leisure. I gather that today London is regarded as one of the 'coolest' cities anywhere for young people. Back in the 1960s I moved to a mews in South Kensington. I was there right at the beginning when King's Road became the centre of the 'Swinging Sixties'. People say that Carnaby Street was the centre, but Kings Road, Chelsea, was the place to walk down!

I love the architecture of London - I love to walk around looking at the upper stories and rooflines of buildings and savouring all the different styles. There was some awful high-rise architecture put up in the 1950s and '60s folowing wartime destruction, but better has followed. Also, many older buildings have been refurbished. I recently attended the re-opening of the Lyceum Theatre, off the Strand - it retains the atmosphere of rather garish Edwardian rococo maroon and gilt decoration, but behind that it is a state-of-the-art, up-to-date theatre.

One of the greatest changes is traffic. As a kid in the East End, in streets of terraced houses, we didn't see cars. I was brought up on all the traditional kids' games - and have since recalled a lot of them in my work - and we could play in the street very safely. Occasionally you would get a brewer's dray, with the barrels of beer and horse-brasses - we used to jump on the back, until the driver's whip came over to dislodge us! There was a lot of dried-up horse manure on the streets - I really miss that smell.

Later, when I could afford a car - pre-traffic meters, pre-yellow lines - I could park outside a club in Piccadilly on a Saturday night without any problem. I used to think I was safe in traffic - I was an East End street boy, it would bounce off me! Today traffic makes such demands on London - it's become a nightmare.

I like certain aspects of pedestrianisation, the way things are now being brought out on to the street. I like street theatre, and I like alfresco restaurants with tables outside - I'm a big people-watcher! The cleaner air is another advantage of modern London. When I was a kid, in the winter there was a lot of black fog, when you couldn't see your hand in front of the your face. If you went out to get a bag of potatoes or a bottle of milk for your mum, when you came back and blew your nose you'd have a black handkerchief! You forget that.

There are still the traffic fumes, of course, but the way to avoid that is to walk along the river, or take a boat. A ride down the Thames really gives you the best perspective on London. It's also the best vantage point from which to appreciate the history of London, and all the villages and individual communities that are what it really is - Chelsea, Westminster, the City. Back in the 1950s I had an idea for a sort of son et lumière trip down the river, projecting aspects of London's history on to the derelict warehouse walls, and having sounds, music and pictures coming from the buildings - a voyage through history. Now the warehouses have gone or have been converted, so it wouldn't work.

I've always loved London, and its history, and feeling a part of that history. There's still something about London that remains in spite of everything that's happening to it - the Londoner's characteristic attitude is something that I cherish, our humour, our ability to laugh at ourselves, our resilience. People ask me why I live in this little street in Acton. It's because it's a neighbourhood; there's a little park, they know me in all the shops, people talk to each other. It's a community, and it reminds me of my childhood. Where I was born in the East End it was a strong Jewish community, and now it's Asian. There were only a couple of Asian families then - one chap sold Indian toffee, like brown candy-floss. Today the families still look after each other in the same way as when I was brought up, but instead of Jewish they're Asian.

There's not as much communal and industrial activity in central London as there was, which I regret, but I'm happy to say that more people are going to the theatre today, which is heartening. I'm hoping to be involved in the Millennium event at Greenwich on the entertainment side - as always, I'm harking back to the time when people went out and had a good time together. London has always been a great entertainment centre, from Vauxhall Gardens in the 18th century to today's vast leisure industry.

Change is necessary and inevitable, even if it's for the worse - and good things *have* been lost. But the London pigeons haven't changed, Nelson still looks out to sea from Trafalgar Square, and I'm certainly optimistic about London's future - as long as we can retain that humour and 'bounceability'.

I've just being accorded the honour of being offered the Freedom of the City of London. I gather that would entitle me to drive a flock of sheep across London Bridge. I might just try that.

INTRODUCTION

In a piece in his 1995 anthology *Writing Home*, Alan Bennett refers to 'that remotest of periods, the recent past', which seems to us to be the ideal justification for the thinking behind this book. It is over 1,900 years since the Roman historian Tacitus described the new settlement of London as 'a celebrated centre of commerce' - which it has, of course, remained ever since - so given that vast canvas, why concentrate on just the past five decades, a mere moment in the capital's history?

There are several reasons. One is related to Alan Bennett's comment. In the latter years of the 20th century our daily lives are so busy, and we live life so fast, that it is impossible to perceive the myriad changes that are occurring all around us every moment of the day. Speed is the watchword - we must travel faster, communicate faster, understand faster. As W. H. Davies wrote in his poem 'Leisure', 'What is life if, full of care, We have no time to stand and stare?' Well, standing and staring is certainly not encouraged in the 1990s! But the further away, the more fixed or set, change becomes - like molten lava cooling on a mountainside - the easier it is to register and come to terms with.

As with the pace of life, so the pace of change is also accelerating. Arguably more has changed during the last 50 years than changed during the previous century. And certainly more has changed during the last 200 years than during the previous 500, and so on. Luckily we now have something to help us record that change more effectively and economically than ever before - the camera. And it is photography that forms the foundation of the 'Past and Present' approach. We can juxtapose a moment caught on film in, say, 1956 with one captured in exactly the same place in 1996. While ideally a whole series of pictures would do the job best - a kind of 'stop-motion' film sequence - a single pair will provide us with that leap back into the recent past, a powerful reminder of all those little details of daily life that we were not even aware that we had forgotten.

It is this minutiae of change that is so absorbing. An example at random - the rubber pressure-pads that used to be set in the road on the approach to traffic lights. Their demise was never publicly announced, there was no overnight replacement, no 'preservation' outcry - but suddenly they were all gone, we didn't notice, and as far as we are concerned we have completely forgotten about them until our memory is stirred by a photograph.

Henry Porter, writing in the *Guardian* newspaper in September 1996 about the inexorable disappearance of our countryside under roads and housing estates, wrote: 'The loss will be imperceptible, rather like the gradual fading of a person's eyesight, and there will be no one moment when we realise what we have done.' Although the context is slightly different, it is an excellent analogy.

This is the other main reason for looking only at the post-war era - nostalgia. The deliberate aim of 'Past and Present' books is to evoke *living memory*. Only a lucky few can remember back to the turn of the last century. Beyond that point nostalgia slips firmly into history - the second-

A memorial to London's wartime firefighters - 'heroes with grimy faces' as Churchill called them - stands outside St Paul's Cathedral, whose dome silhouetted against the flames and smoke of 1940/41 is an enduring image of the spirit of the Blitz and the survival of London against all the odds. *WA*

hand, book-learned past. However, there is no attempt here to be 'rose-tinted'. The 'good old days' frequently weren't. It is its fixed and immutable certainty that makes the past so attractive - nothing will change again, and we can safely overlook its disappointments and shortcomings.

Strictly speaking, 'nostalgia' is supposed to be a painful process, and in a Romantic kind of way perhaps it is. The word is derived from the Greek, and means the 'pain of return' (just as neuralgia means a 'pain in a nerve'). Perhaps some of the following photographs of the capital will be painful, when we see what was needlessly destroyed by war, and what has been destroyed by ignorance and commercial expediency since. Depending on our views on modern architecture, there's some further pain in comparing the old with the new. But who can deny that London's sparkling soot-cleaned buildings, the (relatively) clean air devoid of the notorious 'smogs', and a river once more supporting fish in profusion are not an improvement?

Of course, there is no way of describing the past 50 years in London without reference to at least the previous hundred. By its very nature London has not been subject to such violent change as other cities. The vast majority of its many hundreds of historic sites and buildings survive, carefully and deliberately preserved. Trafalgar Square has not yet been demolished and replaced by an Arndale Centre; St James's Park is not yet an estate of detached executive homes.

In a way the change has been more 'organic'. Even having lived in London for some years, we found during the research for this book that there was more to learn about its history than could ever be absorbed in a single lifetime. Once that was accepted, we began to get an almost tangible sense of the sheer *enormity* of London's past, especially in the City. The overwhelming image is of London as a great forest. Successive architectural, commercial or calamitous 'autumns' have left layers of remains on the 'forest floor', out of which new growth has sprung. Season after season for almost two millennia these strata have been laid down, one above the other, decomposed and regenerated by us industrious human ants! This was brought home to us especially in Poultry, near Mansion House, where a recent archaeological excavation beneath the roots of a modern building project has revealed these layers in the most dramatic way (see pages 66-7). We must also remember that even today's glittering skyscrapers will one day add to London's 'leaf mould' as the seasons turn again. . .

Indeed, this historical continuity makes London a very *physical* place, with such a sense of solid permanence that it is easy to overlook the role of man altogether! Millions of visitors come from around the world to see the sites - the palaces, the parks, the galleries - not the people. London is like a vast temple, and we humans merely its attendants. This has been emphasised in the last 30 years or so by the increasingly 'superhuman' scale of the architecture. For some four centuries the tallest and most symbolic landmark was St Paul's Cathedral - the pinnacle of the 'temple', if you like - standing proudly on the crest of the hill between the valleys of the ancient Fleet and Walbrook rivers. One gets the sense that the old cities of Westminster and London were built by and for ordinary men, on an inspirational yet at the same time accessible scale.

From the 1960s the buildings started to leave behind the man on the ground. Centre Point, the Hilton Hotel and the Post Office (BT) Tower are three well-known examples, culminating in the City with Britain's tallest building, the National Westminster Tower - until superseded by Canary Wharf, which itself may soon be overtaken by the proposed Baltic Exchange 'city in the sky'. St Paul's is now dwarfed, often obscured altogether, by these Titans of commerce. There are no doubt some who would lecture on a text of 'God and Mammon', if both had not already co-habited in the capital for so long.

The motor car has also been an invasive and alienating influence. Traffic congestion and pollution is nothing new to London, of course - the conglomerations of horse-drawn buses and wagons jamming every central street in Victorian and Edwardian photographs demonstrate that. But then the streets were also teeming with people dodging the noisy, malodorous but walking-pace congestion. Increasingly during the period under review the pedestrian, as in every other large city, has been corralled on the pavement by railings, allowed out into traffic-land only when the 'green man' allows it, or banished to unnatural elevated walkways or burrowing subways. Pedestrianisation is an increasingly popular and successful solution, but it is still an unnatural environment forced on us by vehicles that we have created and encouraged, but which are now considered too dangerous for us to be allowed to mingle with. Even the increasingly prevalent bicycle, probably the capital's fastest-moving vehicle, poses a threat to the pedestrian worse than the walking dray-horse of yesteryear!

That is not to say that the motor car holds total sway, which is certainly not the case, as anyone who has tried to drive round London recently will confirm. Draconian traffic management is strictly applied. One-way streets, restricted access, yellow lines, parking meters and traffic wardens have all been part of the London scene for 40 years or more.

Before we leave written impressions for the pictorial comparisons that form the basis of this book, an entertaining sense of five decades of change in the capital can be obtained from tourist guide-books. These comparisons are also, of course, on a much more human level, and demonstrate once again the many post-war developments in daily life that we have assimilated and now take for granted. In other respects they prove the old French adage 'Plus ça change, plus c'est la même chose' - 'The more things change, the more they are the same'! Let's start with traffic.

The Ward Lock 'Red Guide' to London of 1940 offers the following advice: 'Only drivers of nerve and experience should motor in the crowded thoroughfares of London. . . It should be borne in mind that certain **one-way thoroughfares** are closed to all vehicular traffic except that proceeding in a prescribed direction; and that at certain busy spots . . the gyratory or **"roundabout" system** of traffic control is observed: instead of cutting through crossing traffic one turns left and follows the "circus" until the desired turning is reached. By this means much annoying delay is obviated. . . [The] congested state of the streets robs motoring of any pleasure, while the Underground is generally much quicker.

'Owing to traffic congestion the rules regarding car-parking have to be enforced strictly in the busier quarters of London, and before leaving a car standing it is well to consult a policeman concerning the period during which cars may be so left there, if indeed they may be left there at all. . .'

Fifty years later, Louise Nicholson, in her excellent *Definitive Guide to London*, echoes those sentiments: 'Driving in London during weekdays is best avoided. Most of the time is spent in traffic jams, looking for a parking place or trying to master the one-way system to reach a car park. When you give up in desperation and leave the car illegally parked, a parking ticket arrives on the windscreen and a clamp on the wheel. . . Better by far invest in a London travel pass.' (Hear, hear - your authors did just that and it was a very effective and cheap way of getting around! However, walking - or taking a bus if you prefer - is still the best way to get the most from this astonishing city.)

Another marked change evident in many of the photographs is the matter of dress. In 1940 visitors 'desirous of doing in London as Londoners do may welcome a hint or two under this head, though great latitude is allowed, and all varieties of costume may be seen in the streets. For formal calls and social events of importance a black morning coat and silk hat are *de rigueur*, but City and business men are content with lounge suits, and soft felt hats and "bowlers" are generally worn. Evening dress is usual when dining at high-class restaurants. . . At theatres, evening dress is nearly always worn in the boxes and stalls, and generally in the dress circle.'

There's barely a hat to be seen in the 'present' photographs! In 1990, 'In the grand hotels and in the gentlemen's clubs, a jacket and tie is expected. . . If you arrive without, the porter can sometimes lend both. Elsewhere, absolute freedom in theory, but the smarter the restaurant the more it is expected that clients complement the food with dressy clothes.' There's no mention of what to wear to the theatre. . .

In 1940 Lyons and Slaters were recommended for 'a fair light luncheon for 1s 6d or 2s; a dinner from 2s to 5s; while fare of a lighter kind can be had at the shops of the Aerated Bread Co Ltd, J. Lyons & Co Ltd, Express Dairies Co Ltd, Messrs Fuller, and others. . . A number of restaurants catering specially for their own "nationals" - the Indian, Spanish, Chinese, etc - are increasingly patronised by British people accustomed to foreign travel or attracted to novel dishes.' Today, of course, American, Chinese and Indian cuisine is second nature; indeed, the traditional British 'meat and two veg', once a restaurant staple, is virtually unknown.

In 1940 'humble mortals who are content with a "grill", or other simple dish, will pay little more than they would have to do elsewhere.' In the more worldly-wise 1990s, Louise Nicholson recommends the top and bottom of the range of restaurants, but the problem 'is the middle range, where mediocre food and bad service are wickedly overpriced. It is certainly worth doing some research and reading menus in restaurant windows before plunging in.' Choice today is of course far wider even than the 'novel dishes' of 1940s cosmopolitanism: Nicholson lists venues for 'brunch' and the misnamed and trendy newcomer, the 'brasserie', as well as French, Greek, Italian, Japanese and vegetarian restaurants.

If you were satisfied with the fare and service in 1940, and wanted to leave a tip, there were no 'hard and fast rules . . . and the whole system is objectionable, but in hotels of medium standing, 2s 6d per person to the waiter or waitress and about half that sum to the chambermaid is sufficient for a stay of a day or two. . . At restaurants reckon about 1d in the 1s on the bill. . .' In your 1990 hotel or restaurant 'the normal amount is 10-15%. . . Porters would normally expect 50p per suitcase. . .' In 1940 a railway porter might expect 'from 3d to 6d for carrying a hand-bag or rugs, and from 1s for heavy luggage.' No mention is made of railway porters in the 1990 guide. . .

The recent communications revolution leads us to forget the unfamiliarity and rigmarole of making long-distance calls not so long ago. In 1940 'public telephone call office facilities' were provided 'at many post offices, railway sta-

London layers: almost five and a half centuries of London's history in a single photograph. The tower on the right is that of All Hallows Staining, in Mark Lane (between the Tower of London and the Monument). It dates from the mid-15th century (although the church itself was first mentioned in 1177). Repaired in 1630, it survived the Great Fire only to collapse in 1671 due to the excessive number of burials. It was rebuilt, but demolished 200 years later in 1870, except for the tower, which was sold to the Clothworkers' Company for some £12,000 on the understanding that they would maintain it. The building behind is the Clothworkers' Hall of 1955-58, but neo-Georgian (1714-1830) in style. Towering above that is the almost Gothic form of £400 million Minster Court of 1990. How many cities of the world could provide such a juxtaposition? *WA*

tions and shops; and in kiosks. The minimum charge for the use of a call office is 2d. Normally the charge is based upon the radial distance between the exchanges concerned, but details of the charges applicable in London are exhibited in every call office. Trunk (and toll) calls may be effected from practically all public call offices: a call office charge of 2d is payable in addition to the appropriate trunk, etc, charge.

'A message may be dictated from a call office to any post office in the United Kingdom which is a telephone express delivery office for delivery by express messenger, on payment of the appropriate telephone fee for the call (including a call office fee of 2d) plus a writing-down fee of 3d for the first 30 words and 1d for each 10 words or part thereof in excess of 30; plus the express delivery charge of 6d a mile, or part of a mile, from the office of delivery to the addressee.' Phew - thank heavens for fax! By contrast, the 1990 guide gives advice on phonecards, phones that take credit cards, payphones on trains, direct-dialled international calls, and phone services from a morning alarm call to the 24-hour Teledata information service and a Gay Switchboard.

For the tourist, getting to grips with money has also always been important, and this too has changed completely since the war. 'Gold coins (sovereigns and half-sovereigns) have practically disappeared,' says the Red Guide, 'being replaced by **Treasury Notes** of the face value of 20 shillings (green) and ten shillings (brown and slightly smaller). The silver coins are the crown (5s), now very rare; half crown (2s 6d); florin (2s); shilling; sixpence (half a shilling); and "threepenny bits". Be careful to distinguish between half-crowns and florins; the former are larger. Bronze or copper: penny (1d), halfpenny (½d), and farthing (¼d). Farthings are but little used except at draper's establishments and in the poorer districts. Notes are also issued by the Bank of England for sums of £5, £10, £20, £50 and upwards.'

A measure of the changing value of money is the relative rarity of £5 notes in those days. A railway signalman/porter at that time remembers being given a £5 note as a tip by a wealthy passenger: 'It was the first time I had had a fiver, which was white and the size of about half a dozen of today's notes. One had to sign the back of them before they would be accepted as legal tender. The gentleman did mine [joining six or seven signatures already there], and after he had gone I changed it for five ones in the till - a chap of my age with a fiver would have been considered suspicious.' Indeed, when the fiver was discovered in the till the following day, an enquiry as to its origin was instigated, and the railway police even contacted the gentleman concerned to verify the signalman's story! The Red Guide informs us that 'Notes of the value of £5 and upwards paid in [to the Bank of England] are at once cancelled, but are not actually destroyed until a period of five years has elapsed.'

Some readers will become misty-eyed at the nostalgic mention of coins like the half-crown and florin, but the combined effects of inflation and decimalisation saw the end of the farthing as early as 1960, and new 5p and 10p coins were introduced in 1968, supplementing and eventually replacing the shilling and florin coins respectively upon full decimalisation in February 1971. Meanwhile, in 1969 a new 50p coin had replaced the 'ten-bob note'. The halfpenny has subsequently been a casualty, the 5p coin redesigned, the 20p coin introduced, and the £1 coin is a more durable replacement for the bank-note. Even today, more than a quarter of a century after decimalisation, the 'old' (or, to some, 'real') money is remembered with great affection.

A final justification for the post-war time-scale of this book is that London's long history has been punctuated by catastrophes that have proved major turning points in its development. Boadicea sacked and burned the city in AD 60; in 1666 a small fire in a bakehouse destroyed almost 500 acres of the City, including 87 churches and over 13,000 houses, and assured Christopher Wren his place in history; and between September 1940 and May 1941 a third of the City and some 3½ million homes were destroyed in the Blitz. This most recent destruction was the impetus for the capital's current ongoing reincarnation, and provides a good starting point for this comparative study. In fact, the book really starts six years after the war in 1951 with the Festival of Britain, London's - and the nation's - first symbol of post-war renaissance as well as an architectural, commercial and social pointer towards a new era. The fact that in the 1990s plans are already well advanced for Millennium celebrations, including the marking of the 50th anniversary of the Festival in 2001, gives us a convenient near-future landmark as well.

Starting with the Festival site, which was subsequently to be developed as the South Bank arts complex, the book has been designed as an S-shaped perambulation back and forth through Central London: down the river to Tower Bridge; westwards back through the City, Fleet Street/Holborn and the Strand to Trafalgar Square; down Whitehall to Westminster and the seat of Government, and down the Mall to Buckingham Palace and Royal London; to Victoria, north up Park Lane, then eastwards again through the West End to Theatreland and the bright lights of Piccadilly Circus and Leicester Square.

We made this journey over a week in late May 1996, when most of the 'present' photographs were taken, and we keenly recommend that, if you are able, you follow our footsteps on this journey of discovery, book in hand, and hopefully share some of the fascination that we found in what our forebears were proud to call 'the Metropolis of the World'.

1. THE SOUTH BANK

In 1947 the Government set up the Festival Council to plan an event to celebrate the centenary of Prince Albert's 1851 Great Exhibition in the Crystal Palace, as well as to provide a national focus of optimism and rebirth following the dark days of the war. The result was the **FESTIVAL OF BRITAIN** of May-September 1951. '. . .its spirit,' says the introduction to the guide-book, 'will be finding expression in a variety of British sights and a great range of British sounds. Taken together, these will add up to one united act of national reassessment, and one corporate reaffirmation of faith in the nation's future.' It is therefore a good place for us to start this review of developments in the capital since the war.

The site chosen was a parcel of land bounded by Waterloo Bridge (bottom left in the first picture, an aerial postcard view of the Exhibition), Waterloo Station (top left), and County Hall (top right). Notoriously marshy, this land had never been properly developed, and had long presented an eyesore of wharves, timber yards and half-derelict warehouses across the river from the elegant sweep of the Victoria Embankment. A new river wall reclaimed 4½ acres from the river, and the whole site was transformed in not much more than 18 months.

'What the visitor will see on the South Bank,' continues the guide-book, 'is an attempt at something new in exhibitions - a series of sequences of things to look at, arranged in a particular order so as to tell one continuous, interwoven story. The order is important. For the South Bank Exhibition is neither a museum of British culture nor a trade show of British wares; it tells the story of British contributions to world civilisation in the arts of peace. That story has a beginning, a middle, and an end - even if that end consists of nothing more final than fingerposts into the future.'

That future is shown in the third illustration, the planned redevelopment of what is now known as the South Bank Centre. This is intended for completion in 2001, the 50th anniversary of the Festival of Britain. Nicholas Snowman, SBC's Chief Executive: 'What we were looking for, when we began our search for a master planner in February 1994, was a scheme which created a cohesive framework for the activities taking place inside the buildings, one which would unite us with the north bank of London, across the psychological divide of the river. . . Richard Rogers and his team have given us a visionary concept which achieves that - and goes beyond it - to create a spirit of celebration and a new landmark for London.'

This £167 million vision includes a new futuristic 'Skylon', the 1951 original having been a striking symbol of the Festival, a new river bridge with shops and catering, a refurbished Royal Festival Hall, two floating 'eyots' beneath the bridges, with restaurants, etc, and a new 'Crystal Palace'. This latter was described by Deyan Sudjic in *The Guardian* as 'nothing short of a visionary proposal for burying the squalor and concrete of the South Bank with a tidal wave of glass . . . the kind of spectacular concept that simply doesn't happen in Britain any more.' The canopy will span and unite the various concert halls to create a new plaza - 'a "people's palace" for the 21st century'. *Authors' collection (2)/map by Grundy & Northedge, courtesy South Bank Centre*

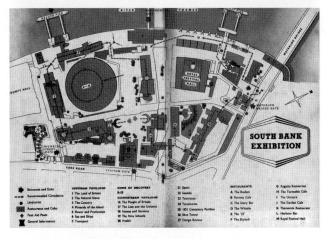

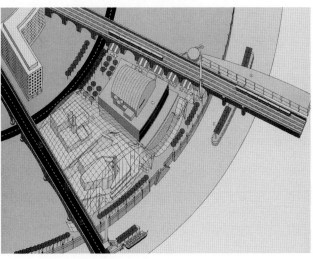

Opposite page The only original structure on the site to be preserved as part of the Exhibition was the **SHOT TOWER**, built in 1826 (see also page 26). Molten lead was dropped from the melting chamber at the top, forming perfect spheres as it fell the 120 feet into cold water at the bottom. As recently as the 1930s about 10 tons of shot was made there in a day. Not yet fitted to the top of the tower in this 1951 photograph (but seen in the picture on page 17) is the lighthouse that flashed to welcome visitors 'as far as 45 miles away when the weather is clear'; the lens was made by the same firm that had made the glass for the Crystal Palace in 1851. In addition there was a radio beacon, connected to a radio telescope in the Dome of Discovery, by means of which '. . .visitors can transmit signals to the moon and actually see them reflected back to earth after about two and half seconds'. St Paul's can be seen in the distance.

The Shot Tower was subsequently demolished to make way for the Queen Elizabeth Hall of 1967, seen beyond the corner of the Royal Festival Hall in the 1996 photo, together with the new Riverside Walk and raised terraces that replaced the original Festival gardens and the strange 'bowsprit' balconies projecting into the river from in front of the 'Seaside' exhibit. A year before the Festival opened there was only one tree on the site - a further 60 were brought in and planted. The characteristic 'London plane' trees of today give the area a more permanent feel; note the flaking of the trees' bark, a habit that may account for its ability to resist the once sooty atmosphere of this and many other cities. *Frank Hornby/WA*

This page The **ROYAL FESTIVAL HALL** itself, so named at the request of King George VI, was the only permanent building on the Exhibition site and was built under the auspices of the then London County Council, whose crest is seen above the name in this 25 June 1955 photograph. The design was begun in 1948, and the building opened in 1951 ready for the Festival; the first concerts in May were conducted by such great names of the day as Sir Adrian Boult and Sir Malcolm Sargent. It was the first major British public building designed in the contemporary architectural style; the concert hall itself nestled in the centre, surrounded by circulating areas, restaurants, etc, hence the large glazed screens on the river front.

Then in 1962 the frontage was extended 30 feet towards the river, and the original idiosyncratic appearance of the hall was lost. The main restaurant and foyer were enlarged and replanned, the side elevations simplified, and more extensive elevated walkways built, giving the wider, more neutral appearance seen in the 'present' view, now increasingly obscured by those plane trees. *C. F. B. Penley, A. Mott collection/WA*

Opposite page The tour of the Exhibition began with 'The Land of Britain', the pavilion entered by the curious bonnet-like structure seen in the left middle distance. The building dominating this view, however, is the **DOME OF DISCOVERY**, 365 feet in diameter; the photograph was taken from the cab of a locomotive on Hungerford railway bridge on 2 June 1951. One of the most important aspects of the Exhibition was that is was planned as a totally informal and asymmetrical group of buildings. They were different heights, on different levels with different-sized areas between them. The groundscape varied from slabs to cobbles, flowers in tubs to pools and fountains, all modern details that were to influence New Town planning at such places as Harlow and Stevenage.

'The great story of British Discovery,' says the guide-book, 'is related in the huge aluminium saucer of the Dome of Discovery, a structure which is as adventurous, fantastic and technically triumphant as the history of British Discovery itself.' On the right is the 296-foot-high 'Skylon'.

In 1863 Britain - indeed, London - gave the world the first underground railway, and it is the works for the extension of the Jubilee Line from Charing Cross to Docklands that occupy part of the Festival site today (see also page 111). The site has remained strangely neglected and undeveloped, having once destined for the National Theatre until the mid-1960s, and is currently occupied by a car and coach park and the Jubilee Gardens of 1977. A modern crane imitates the 'Skylon', and the roofline of County Hall can be seen in the top left-hand corner of both pictures. *Neil Davenport/WA*

This page This interesting view in what is today **BELVEDERE ROAD** dates from 22 September 1951 and is looking eastwards back towards the railway that bisected the site. Beyond it the Royal Festival Hall can be clearly seen, as well as the Shot Tower with its special top (see page 14). The large glazed building in front of the railway is the 'Transport' pavilion. On the left is the Dome of Discovery, and on the right 'The Country', containing exhibits of livestock and agricultural machinery, forestry and rural crafts, as well as 'The Dairy Bar', selling milk 'in cartons, for drinking at or near the bar' - a litter precaution?

On the left of the 1996 view are the Jubilee Gardens, and on the right the foot of the Shell Tower, completed in 1963, and the viewing gallery of which we shall be visiting shortly. *Arthur Davenport/WA*

This page Moving now to the other end of the South Bank complex, this 2 May 1963 view from Waterloo Bridge shows the site cleared for the **QUEEN ELIZABETH HALL**, **PURCELL ROOM** and **HAYWARD GALLERY**. The background is dominated by part of the newly completed Shell Centre, the 10-storey L-shaped block on the north side of the railway, and part of a similar U-shaped block on the other side, with the bottom of its 26-storey tower just visible. Already beneath the arches of the bridge is the National Film Theatre (1956-8), whose sign can be seen directing people down the steps.

Something that the new 2001 development of the South Bank Centre seeks to address is the rather forbidding bleakness of the relentless shuttered concrete and paving, seen in the 1996 view of the finished complex. The Queen Elizabeth Hall and Purcell Room (right) has walls and roof of concrete, with no break between them. It has few windows, but exposed ducts. 'It is a thrilling experience if the weather is fine and you are at leisure,' says architectural historian Sir Nikolaus Pevsner. 'But what if it rains, what if you are late, what if you find steps a strain?' One of the design team for the Festival Hall said in 1967, '. . .it expresses its component parts in oddly shaped volumes cast in concrete. . . For the visual excitement . . . one has to accept a bedraggled look on a rainy day.' The 'black

hole' under the walkways contains service roads, car parks and thundering skateboarders - certainly not a welcoming environment late at night. The NFT has also now been joined by the excellent Museum of the Moving Image. *Arthur Davenport/WA*

This page Swinging the camera round to the right, this view, on the same day, shows work in progress for the front extension of the **ROYAL FESTIVAL HALL** The foundations are laid, the external walkways removed and temporary steps provided from Hungerford footbridge. It is interesting to note how stained by weather (and smoke?) the Festival Hall has become in 12 years,

compared with how much better the new frontage appears to have fared in the ensuing 33 years. What look to be fairly temporary flower beds are still being built on what had been the site of the 'Sport' pavilion.

Today's view had to be taken from further out on the bridge to avoid the trees, but shows the new river face of the Royal Festival Hall to good advantage, together with the modern Festival Pier, which has replaced the 'Rodney Pier' of 1951. The skyline remains remarkably unchanged apart from the intrusion behind Big Ben of the three blocks of the Department of the Environment (ironically!) of 1963-71. *Neil Davenport/WA*

2. SHELL TOWER PANORAMA

Above The whole of the Shell complex on the South Bank is seen here approaching completion in September 1962. Following completion of the 26-storey, 338-foot tower of the Shell Building the following year, the viewing gallery afforded stupendous panoramic views across London. Today building work and security considerations mean that the gallery is completely closed, but we are grateful to Shell for allowing photographer Colin Whyman access to the gallery to take the following 'present' photographs. *Frank Hornby*

Opposite page One tends to think of the Thames as passing through London from west to east, but this first pair of views upstream is actually looking almost due south. The dates are 18 May 1963 and June 1996.

The building in the right foreground is County Hall, begun as the headquarters of the erstwhile London County Council in 1912 and completed in 1922, having been interrupted by the First World War. As can be seen, the offices are set around courtyards faced with white glazed tiles, with the Council Chamber in the centre. A more modern extension of the offices is just being completed on the left in 1963.

The large Victorian complex of buildings beyond Westminster Bridge is St Thomas's Hospital, of 11th century origin but named after 12th-century martyr St Thomas à Becket. Queen Victoria laid the foundation stone on this new site in 1868 and opened the hospital in 1871. The north end of the complex was badly bombed during the war, and a broken edge of building can be seen in the 1963 view just above the roof of County Hall, while the new East Wing is seen under construction on the left. In 1969-76 the new north block was built, a white cube contrasting severely with the remaining Victorian buildings.

In the distance, beyond Lambeth Bridge on the west bank, is Millbank Tower (see page 32), then the three 1928 Edwardian-style blocks housing ICI and government offices. In the distance can be seen Battersea Power Station of 1929-35; it chimneys are still smoking in 1963, but it finally closed in 1983.

Two particular contrasts between the two views are the growth of the trees, outside the rear of County Hall and on both sides of the river, and the present-day cleanness of the buildings (including the Houses of Parliament, extreme right). *Frank Hornby/Colin Whyman*

We now swing the camera round towards the south-west to look at Westminster Bridge and the Houses of Parliament, the 'past' picture dating from the late 1960s, with the three 200-foot-high slabs of the Department of the Environment under construction in the left background. Note that both pictures were taken at exactly 2.10 pm.

Already the area round Victoria is built up with tower blocks, several more having joined them in the following 30 years. The tower of Westminster (RC) Cathedral is right

of centre in the distance, and to its right can be seen the nearer domed roof of the Methodist Central Hall. Nearer still, on the corner of Bridge Street and Victoria Embankment, demolition of a block of buildings for redevelopment and to aid the construction of the Jubilee Line extension is perhaps the biggest difference between the two pictures.

At the extreme right, on the Embankment, is New Scotland Yard, familiar as the headquarters of the Metropolitan Police. Originally the Met's headquarters were in Great Scotland Yard, towards the top of Whitehall next to Trafalgar Square. When these new premises were built in 1890, appropriately built with granite dug by Dartmoor convicts, they were named New Scotland Yard. Then in 1967 a move was made to a third head-quarters off Victoria Street, bearing the same name but which perhaps should have been *New* New Scotland Yard! This is the 20-storey block with the black upper floor most clearly seen in the 1960s photograph between Westminster Cathedral and Central Hall. Note again how much cleaner the Houses of Parliament are today, while St Margaret's Church and Westminster Abbey beyond positively gleam in their new-found whiteness! Queen Boadicea on her chariot can just be glimpsed at the west end of Westminster Bridge, above the steps leading down to Westminster Pier with its pleasure and ferry boats. *C. F. B. Penley, A. Mott collection/Colin Whyman*

We are now looking due west, and there is very little difference between these two views, the 'past' one taken on 9 August 1967 and the 'present' nearly 30 years later. For here we looking over Government London and Royal London, left largely unscathed by the war and still displaying all the architectural pomp and circumstance of the administrative heart of the nation. Note again though how virtually every major building in view has been cleaned, losing the unsightly soot-stains of previews. Clean Air Act London.

In the centre of the pictures, on Victoria Embankment, is the Royal Air Force Memorial of 1923, surmounted by its gold eagle. Behind it is the rather severe block of the Ministry of Defence building, designed in 1913 but only completed in the late 1950s. Its utilitarian

walls with their plain windows and strange east-west upper blocks, likened by Pevsner to 'two-storeyed houses . . stranded high up', led him to describe the building as a 'monument of tiredness'. Certainly it contrasts unfavourably with the buildings on the right, Whitehall Court of 1884, with all its Victorian exuberance.

Immediately to the left of the Ministry of Defence, and on the far side of Whitehall, is Downing Street, the roofs of which can just be seen. To its left is the square block of the Foreign Office, and above it the frontage of Buckingham Palace at the far end of St James's Park. Diagonally back towards Whitehall runs The Mall, shrouded in trees, bounded at its right-hand end by the white facade of Carlton House Terrace. The tall building in the centre background is the Hilton Hotel. *C. F. B. Penley, A. Mott collection/Colin Whyman*

The view is now rather more to the north-west, the foreground dominated by Hungerford Bridge. The pre-Victoria Embankment engraving of 1845 has been included because it shows several things of interest. The foreground shows the south bank as it used to be, a jumble of wharves, warehouses and timber yards. Prominent on the right is the Shot Tower (see page 14), and to its left the Lion Brewery, built at about the same time (1826). The lions on it were made of Coade, an artificial stone once made at a factory on the site of County Hall (left of the picture); one of them, made in 1837, was removed when the brewery was demolished in 1949, was displayed at the Festival of Britain and is now to be seen at the east end of Westminster Bridge outside County Hall.

The original Hungerford Bridge was, as can be seen, a suspension footbridge, built in 1841-5. This was removed (and the chains used in Bristol's Clifton Suspension Bridge) when the railway bridge was built in 1863 to carry the South Eastern Railway into Charing Cross station. The new bridge used cast-iron cylinders as well as the old bridge's two main red-brick piers, as seen in the photographs.

The bridge was some 61 feet wide and carried four railway tracks; because Victoria Embankment did not then exist, nothing more than functional engineering was thought necessary. Footpaths were provided on both sides to replace the suspension bridge. In 1887 the bridge was widened by nearly 50 feet on the upstream (left) side, which again can be seen in the photographs. In 1905 the original lofty arched roof of the station collapsed during maintenance work, and was replaced by the ridge-and-furrow roof seen in the 9 August 1967 photo.

The bridge's functional ugliness was to cause controversy. Before the war, Arthur Mee, in *The King's England*, described it as 'the ugliest thing seen on the Thames', a 'foul structure sprawling across the river on something like huge drainpipes'. As early as

1889 a new elegant road bridge was envisaged; the station would be moved to the south bank, allowing widening of the Strand. The railway company was not keen, however, even though the bridge was no longer strong enough to allow more than two tracks to be used at a time, and then only with lightweight locomotives. During the First World War there were plans to strengthen the bridge with new piers and metal arches, but nothing happened until a Royal Commission in 1926 recommended a double-decker bridge, road above rail. In 1928 a road bridge alone was again the favoured option, a plan presented to what was by then the Southern Railway as a matter of national importance; the site of the Lion Brewery was offered for the new terminus. All was agreed, but in 1930 Parliament rejected the idea! In 1936 the double-deck idea raised its ugly head once more, but the Second World War effectively killed all discussion, and 'that ugly red-oxide Behemoth which sprawls from the north to the south' remains today, subject to 1990s plans by the South Bank Centre for an additional footbridge with shops, etc.

Charing Cross station itself has been the subject of dramatic change since 1967. In the late 1980s the value of the air space above the station platforms was realised by the BR Property Board, the result being the massive and rather striking development straddling the platforms today, known as No 1 Embankment Place. Above the Embankment the over-track 1888 signal box has also been lost with automation of the signalling, and the rationalisation of the track layout has enabled lengthening of one of the platforms.

Dominating the skyline are the Post Office Tower (now British Telecom Tower) and Centre Point (see page 105), while on the river in 1996 work is in progress on the new Charing Cross Pier (see pages 38-39). *Authors' collection/C. F. B. Penley, A. Mott collection/Colin Whyman*

We're now looking more or less north, across the South Bank Centre and Waterloo Bridge towards Aldwych and Fleet Street. The first view, dating from the early to mid-1960s, shows the Queen Elizabeth Hall and Hayward Gallery under construction, and on the other side of the bridge what was to become the site of the National Theatre. Prominent at the north end of the bridge is Brettenham House of 1930-32, then across the road to the right is Somerset House. This was started in 1776 as purpose-built offices for government departments on the site of the house of the Duke of Somerset, Protector of the boy king Edward VI, who met his end in the Tower before it was completed. The new building's 800-foot-long river frontage used to stand above and have access from the Thames before the Embankment was built in front of it. Behind it is the Strand and Aldwych, and further to the right the thin, dark spire of the Royal Courts of Justice. The ships

moored on the Thames are the dark hull of Shackleton's polar exploration ship *Discovery*, and the white hull of HQS *Wellington*, the floating livery hall of the Honourable Company of Master Mariners (see also page 45).

By the date of the second photograph, 9 August 1967, the new South Bank buildings are freshly completed, the Hayward Gallery distinguished by its pyramid skylights. The National Theatre site can be seen more clearly, being used as a coach and car park.

By 1996 the National Theatre is built and trees mask its severe outline from the river. On the far bank the major change is the new buildings for King's College (University of London), next door to Somerset House, completed in 1971. *Discovery* has been removed to Dundee. *David Keane/C. F. B. Penley, A. Mott collection/ Colin Whyman*

Looking slightly north-east now, the panorama is directly towards the City, and in 1967 the south bank between Waterloo and Blackfriars bridges is still lined by wharves, warehouses and the occasional crane. This stretch of the Thames is known as King's Reach, named as part of King George V's Jubilee celebrations in 1935. The curved L-shaped building in the foreground is part of the Shell Centre (seen also on page 19), then beyond the southern approach to Waterloo Bridge in 1996 is the National Theatre. Beyond that, replacing the warehouses along Upper Ground, are today the premises of IBM, followed by the tower of the South Bank Television Centre. Approximately on this site was Barge House Street, site of the sheds once used to house the Royal barges. Even fairly modern-looking buildings on the south side of the street have been demolished, while the end of the street is dominated by the massive King's Reach development of flats, shops and hotel, begun in 1970 and swallowing up the 'OXO' tower (see page 44). Obscured today are Blackfriars road and railway bridges. Look how the City skyline has sprouted in the last 30 years - of which more later! *C. F. B. Penley, A. Mott collection/Colin Whyman*

Our final view is just slightly to the right of the one opposite, taking in even more of today's dramatic City skyline, amidst which the Thames has completely disappeared from this angle! In the foreground in the former 'Royal Waterloo Hospital for Children', moved here in 1822, and this building dating from 1903-5; it currently houses the Schiller International University. The view is along Stamford Street, laid out in the 1790s across Lambeth Marsh, towards King's Reach Tower; the engineer John Rennie, designer of the original Waterloo and Southwark Bridges, lived here in the early part of the last century. At the end, near Rennie Street, are the headquarters of J. Sainsbury, the supermarket giant. Note how the large light-coloured warehouse in the middle distance had been replaced very recently by a block of small houses - surely an enlightened move.

Now let's return to ground level and walk down the river from Millbank to the Tower. *C. F. B. Penley, A. Mott collection/Colin Whyman*

3. THE THAMES AND ITS BRIDGES

Our journey down the river begins at **MILLBANK**, seen here from the Albert Embankment on the south bank of the river just upstream of Lambeth Bridge. Note the characteristic riverside lamp standard, with the entwined dolphins at its base, one of many modelled for the new Albert and Victoria Embankments in 1870, and reproduced since for new work. Also linking the two views is Millbank Tower, seen in the 'past' view on 21 January 1961 under construction; it was built for the Vickers Group and completed in 1963. With 32 floors and a height of 387 feet, its concave/convex glazed sides give it a much lighter feel than its slightly lower but contemporary rival the Shell Tower.

A little to the left can be seen the domed roof of the Tate Gallery, built in 1897 on the site of Millbank Penitentiary, a prison completed in 1821 when Millbank (where Westminster Abbey's mill stood in the 16th century) was muddy, marshy wasteground. The building on the extreme right, now thoroughly cleaned, is Thames House (1928), containing government offices.
C. F. B. Penley, A. Mott collection/WA

This majestic view of the Houses of Parliament from **LAMBETH BRIDGE** has changed little since the building was finally completed in 1860, except for the cleaning of the stonework bringing its superb Gothic lines into sharper relief.

The other subtle difference between the two views is the state of the tide. Twice a day the Thames rises and falls over 7 metres in the vicinity of the anti-flood barrier across the river at Woolwich, and even this far upstream the difference can be clearly seen when one looks at the supports for Lambeth Pier and the piers of Westminster Bridge in the background. The building on the pier seems to have been replaced by a larger one since the 'past' picture was taken on 24 September 1955.

The river is also, of course, much cleaner than it was, even in recent years. During the hot summer of 1858 came 'the Great Stink'; the Speaker of the House of Commons said, 'They had built . . . a magnificent palace for the legislature, but how could they direct the attention of any foreigner to it, when he would be welcomed by a stench which was overpowering?' River excursions were stopped and Parliament's windows draped with sheets soaked in chloride of lime. In the 1860s better drainage began to improve the situation, and the open sewer that was the Thames is now cleaner than it has been for 200 years; in 1974 a salmon was caught in it, the first since about 1840. The Thames now supports 114 fish species, and heron and cormorant are moving into central London. One cause for concern, though, is that the continual narrowing and constraining of the river between vertical walls (in Roman times it was hundreds of yards wide) is threatening this new habitat and increasing the risk of flooding.

Incidentally, until the first Westminster Bridge was opened in 1750 the only places to cross the Thames were by London Bridge or the horse ferry here at Millbank. The considerable sum of £25,000 compensation was paid to the watermen when Westminster Bridge was built, and several thousand to the Archbishop of Canterbury, who owned the ferry rights. *Frank Hornby/WA*

Adjacent to Lambeth Bridge is **LAMBETH PALACE**, which has been the residence of the Archbishops of Canterbury since the 12th century, so it is perhaps not surprising that little has changed in this historic corner of London in the last 40 years! The fine Tudor brick-built gatehouse is known as Morton's Tower; behind it is the Hall, whose great hammerbeam roof had to be restored following wartime damage. To the right is the church of St Mary-at-Lambeth. In olden days, before the Embankment was built, the Palace was approached directly from the river, where Lambeth Pier now stands. Note the naval vessel moored on the right in the September 1956 photograph, while an ice-cream van and tourist coaches are prominent in 1996. *Frank Hornby/WA*

Two of the south bank's earliest notable buildings are seen together in this view from 20 April 1957, **ST THOMAS'S HOSPITAL** and **COUNTY HALL**. St Thomas's was built in 1868-71 on the 'block' or 'pavilion' principle popular on the Continent and approved by Florence Nightingale (who established her Nightingale Training School of Nursing here and revolutionised the profession). The idea was to allow maximum ventilation and air circulation. There were originally seven pavilions ranged along the 1,666-foot length of the building, each with three wards above a service floor, but following war damage and subsequent demolition at the northern end of the site, only the three southern blocks remain. As we have already seen on pages 20-21, the new block, completed in 1976, sits awkwardly alongside the Victorian original. Note how the trees have grown along this first section of public promenade to be built on the south bank.

The design of County Hall, to be the headquarters of the London County Council, was put out to competition in 1908, but it was not until 1922 that the southern end of the building was completed. The river frontage is 700 feet long, with a large concave colonnade in the centre. During the construction a sunken Roman barge was found in the mud, now on display at the London Museum. The LCC became the Greater London Council in 1965, then the GLC was abolished in 1986, leaving London as the only major European capital without an overall controlling authority. County Hall was offered for sale, and in 1992 was sold to Japanese millionaire Takashi Shirayama for £60 million, who in turn sold on

a lease to the Whitbread Group who are to convert the building into two hotels, one luxury and one budget, by 1998. Further controversy was fuelled when the Japanese owner refused to allow ex-servicemen to hold a remembrance service at the building's war memorial. In 1997 The London Aquarium was opened in the basement; it is one of Europe's largest, and London's first, exhibits of live fish and marine life. *Frank Hornby/WA*

This Victorian engraving of the original **WESTMINSTER BRIDGE** in 1754 is included to give an impression of what Westminster looked like before the present Palace of Westminster was built (1837-58) after the original buildings were destroyed by fire in 1834. Westminster Hall, the turreted building at the end of the bridge, was the only building to survive the fire, and was incorporated in the new Palace of Westminster.

In the second view, taken from the terrace in front of County Hall some time in the mid-1960s, the dour appearance of the soot-blackened buildings is obvious; the roof of Westminster Abbey can be seen beyond, as in the 1754 picture. In the background the new New Scotland Yard tower is under construction.

The first Westminster Bridge, built of masonry, had opened in 1750; no dogs were allowed and anyone defacing the walls was threatened with death! There were, however, problems with the foundations, and the present cast-iron bridge was constructed in 1854-62; its great width of 84 feet was most unusual at the time.

In May 1996 access to the terrace was not possible because of the building work on County Hall, and the bridge itself was also undergoing major strengthening work, due for completion in October 1997, so a slightly different angle was required. However, the clock shows the same time, 9.30 am! The building work on the corner of the Embankment can be clearly seen. *Authors' collection/David Keane/WA*

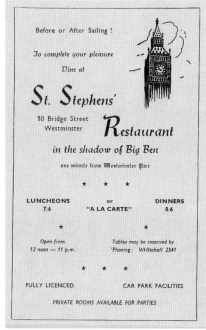

On the Thames beside the bridge is Westminster Pier. The 1940 Red Guide advises: 'A number of steam and motor boats make daily passages during the summer from Westminster Bridge to Kew, Richmond, Hampton Court, etc. Luncheon and tea are served on board at moderate prices.' Alternatively luncheons and dinners could be had at St Stephens Restaurant in Bridge Street (*above*). Today boats still leave the pier for those destinations, as well as a regular service down river to Greenwich. In June 1988 a service of seven 62-seater river buses was started from Chelsea to Greenwich at intervals of 20 to 30 minutes, but this service seems subsequently to have been discontinued.

Hungerford Bridge has already been described on pages 26-7, and this is the view from its western end, looking down on **CHARING CROSS PIER**, a regular stopping place for trips up and down the river, at 11.32 am on 24 September 1955 and 21 March 1997. The 'present' view shows that the pier has been moved pending work by the Port of London Authority, which controls 70 miles of the river from Teddington to the estuary, to install a new pier pontoon with waiting areas and offices, mooring 'dolphins' (piles or buoys), ticket office and three access 'brows' (gangways) from the Embankment. In the meantime a temporary pier is being used a little way downstream.

Of the buildings prominent in the background, the one on the left is the New Adelphi. The original Adelphi was an ambitious scheme by the architects James, John and Robert Adam ('Adelphi' is Greek for 'brothers'). They leased the land in the 1770s and built the first of London's great riverside compositions - a quay and vaults at river level surmounted by four streets of elegant brick houses. It was not a success and nearly bankrupted the brothers, and was then altered and spoiled in the Victorian era. In 1936 the central portion was demolished and replaced by the building seen here - 'savagely ungraceful', as Pevsner describes it. Since 1955 it seems to have gained a couple of extra storeys, improving its appearance a little.

Next door is the bulk of Shell-Mex House (1931), originally the Cecil Hotel facing the Strand, which opened in 1886 as Europe's largest with 800 bedrooms. Pevsner calls it, accurately, 'thoroughly unsubtle'. Beyond is the Savoy Hotel. *Frank Hornby/WA*

Although Wordsworth wrote his famous sonnet from Westminster Bridge in 1802, today this view of **WATERLOO BRIDGE** and the river bend from Hungerford Bridge looking towards St Paul's and the City is as good as any.

> 'Earth hath not anything to show more fair;
> Dull would he be of soul who could pass by
> A sight so touching in its majesty:
> This City doth like a garment wear
> The beauty of the morning: silent, bare,
> Ships, towers, domes, theatres, and temples lie
> Open unto the fields, and to the sky,
> All bright and glittering in the smokeless air. . .'

Well, London was to see more than its fair share of smoke and squalor in the century and a half that followed, but thanks to the Clean Air Act of 1956, by 22 October 1964 the vista from Hungerford Bridge once again 'glitters in the smokeless air'. A further Clean Air Act followed in 1968, and today the dramatic reduction in air pollutants has left the main problem that of vehicle emissions.

Originally referred to as Strand Bridge, the first Waterloo Bridge, by John Rennie, was opened on the second anniversary of the battle, 18 June 1817, and is seen in the 1845 engraving on pages 26-7. In 1923 two of its piers settled badly, and a temporary bridge had to be built alongside. After long controversy and protests the old bridge was demolished in 1936, and the new wider one, of cantilevered concrete box girders, constructed in 1937-42.

A pre-war guide-book says that from this vantage point the dome of St Paul's is well seen, and allows the observer 'to appreciate Wren's masterly grouping of spires in relation to it'. Even by 1964 the spires are being obscured by taller, bulkier buildings; by 28 May 1969, the date of the second photograph, six or more further blocks have sprung up, and by 1997 St Paul's is well and truly dwarfed! The tallest of the buildings in the 'present' view is the National Westminster Tower, begun in 1971 and completed in 1980. It has 52 floors and at 600 feet was Europe's tallest building until superseded by Canary Wharf, 250 feet taller; at the time of writing it is undergoing refurbishment and all its 150,000 sq ft stand empty.

In September 1996 a yet taller tower was announced, Britain's first 1,000-feet-plus skyscraper, on the site of the Baltic Exchange in the City, badly damaged in the IRA bomb attack in 1992. Designed by Sir Norman Foster, its 90 floors would make it one-third as high again as Canary Wharf, it would house 10,000 people in hotels, penthouses and offices, and would have 'parks in the sky' at 20-storey intervals, restaurants and recreation areas. Dubbed the 'erotic gherkin' because of its unconventional curvaceous appearance, the proposal suffered a setback in January 1997 following a plan by English Heritage, the Government's advisers, to limit new buildings in London to no more than 100 metres (320 feet), well below even the NatWest Tower. It remains to be seen whether in any event the new tower would find tenants amongst the many other empty office blocks in London (in 1996 11 per cent of the total commercial floorspace in the central business area remained vacant). *Arthur Davenport (2)/WA*

Less glittering - in fact, rather misty - is this view from the other end of Hungerford Bridge of what today is known as **FESTIVAL PIER**, outside the Royal Festival Hall (see also page 19). Dated 8 January 1954, it shows the curious elevated riverside platforms to good effect (see page 14) and what had been known during the Exhibition as 'Rodney Pier'. From this angle high-rise develop-ment has not affected the skyline on the north bank. A new ship has appeared, moored beneath Waterloo Bridge. This is *Queen Mary II*, which back in 1954 was sailing out of the Clyde on cruises to such places as the Kyles of Bute. Built in 1933 as *Queen Mary*, the 'II' was added at the request of Cunard when the latter's rather larger ship was launched in 1936! *Arthur Davenport/WA*

Crossing back to the north bank, we are now standing on **WATERLOO BRIDGE** above the Victoria Embankment, looking down on the floating station of the Thames Police; in both the 'past' (20 July 1958) and 'present' pictures, police launches are in evidence. At the beginning of the 19th century the huge trade being conducted around the Upper and Lower Pools, with as many as 8,000 ships moored within 6 miles, afforded endless possibilities for theft, and the docks organised their own polic-

ing until it was unified under the Port of London Authority in 1909. In 1839 the official River Police had been absorbed into the Metropolitan force to become the Met's Thames Division, which today is based at Wapping.

As observed on pages 28-9, the ship *Discovery* has moved, as has HMS *Chrysanthemum*, formerly moored between HQS *Wellington* and HMS *President*. The trees have sprouted, and so have the skyscrapers! *Arthur Davenport/WA*

Moving to the other (south) end of **WATERLOO BRIDGE**, we are now looking downstream along King's Reach from the site of the National Theatre. As we have already seen from the aerial views (pages 28-9), a vacant site existed downstream of the bridge, although until 1967 the theatre was intended to be next door to County Hall. Whatever, the river wall was being extended and the shore and derelict land within being enclosed as early as 2 May 1963, as seen in the first photograph. The narrow dock and chimney clearly belong to an earlier age, and the rickety wooden jetty appears to be in course of demolition. Note the brick wall behind the chimney, for by 14 January 1965 the new granite river wall has been extended round to it, and the area behind filled and levelled.

Today the wall has been extended again to provide an unbroken sweep of riverside walk planted with trees as far as that other famous London theatre, Shakespeare's Globe, in the shadow of the former Bankside Power Station, whose chimney can be seen smoking in the two 'past' views, but is now out of sight behind the trees. *Neil Davenport (2)/WA*

A **NATIONAL THEATRE** has been the subject of speculation and discussion for over a century. In the early 1900s the initiative came from Stratford-upon-Avon and the Shakespeare Memorial National Theatre Committee, who held meetings, launched appeals and kept the idea alive for several decades. Sites were acquired then discarded in Bloomsbury and South Kensington; indeed, four different foundation stones were laid. After the war a National Theatre Fund granted £1 million for the project under a commission co-chaired by Sir Laurence Olivier. In 1951 a foundation stone was laid on a site between County Hall and the Royal Festival Hall, and Sir Denys Lasdun was appointed architect. The idea was almost abandoned in 1961, then in 1962 a National Theatre Company was set up, with Olivier as its Artistic Director and the Old Vic as its base. In 1975 Sir Peter Hall took over, and in 1976 the company was able to move into its new home, which in the end was built on the site downstream of Waterloo Bridge.

The theatre actually comprises three auditoria, the Cottesloe (the smallest, named after the Chairman of the National Theatre Board), the Lyttelton (the family name of Lord Chandos, Chairman of the South Bank Theatre Board), and the Olivier (the largest). Building began in about 1969, and the first view (2 June 1971) shows the early stages (and also the base of the South Bank Television Centre tower).

Eleven months later the latter building is almost complete, the block of the fly-tower for the Lyttelton (right) is finished, and the main tower, that for the Olivier (centre, set diagonally to the main building) is nearing completion.

The finished building is seen on 26 May 1978, its concrete facing, marked as in other buildings on the South Bank with the grain of the board shuttering used in its construction, still bright and sharp. 'The various towers and turrets,' says Pevsner, 'form themselves into ever-varying patterns.' Notwithstanding, the Prince of Wales added it to his list of dislikes, comparing it to a nuclear power station, but Sir Peter Hall still loves it: 'It's one of the few architectural successes of modern London. . . Buildings, and especially theatres, need to be allowed to grow old, but I think that we are still too close, we don't have enough of a perspective, we should let it go for another 20 years before doing too much to it.' Unfortunately, the effects of weather have turned the building a dreary grey colour, although today the mature trees along the river help to soften the bleakness. *All Neil Davenport*

Opposite page Here's **KING'S REACH** again, from near the north end of Waterloo Bridge, showing the warehouses that once lined the bank. The date is 3 August 1957, and the tide is well out; note that the warehouse seen in earlier views under the name of 'Daily Mail' was previously 'News Chronicle', a national daily that closed in 1960. In the far distance can be seen the forest of cranes around the Upper Pool, and the top of the Monument.

Dominating the skyline are the distinctive single chimney of Bankside Power Station and the 'OXO' tower. Sir Giles Gilbert Scott's power station was brand new in 1957, and was built to burn oil rather than coke. Now redundant, the 500-foot turbine hall is to be converted between 1997 and 2000 at a cost of £100 million into the Tate Gallery's new Gallery of Modern Art to house the work of artists ranging from Andy Warhol to Henry Moore. In

the 'present' view its chimney just pokes above the King's Reach flats adjacent to Blackfriars Bridge.

The Oxo warehouse dates from 1928, its architectural embellishments cunningly advertising the product from every angle! It has survived the surrounding redevelopment, and recently Oxo Tower Wharf has been converted into an area of little craft shops, workshops and restaurants, accessible from the new riverside path, The Queen's Walk. After years of dereliction, the buildings around the tower itself re-opened in September 1996 as a food and design centre, including the Harvey Nichols restaurant on the top floor overlooking the river. River pleasure boats can be seen in the foreground of both pictures, while the backdrop of the 1996 view is once again the South Bank Television Centre and King's Reach Tower. *Frank Hornby/WA*

This page The north end of **VICTORIA EMBANKMENT** is seen from the south end of Waterloo Bridge on the same day, 3 August 1957, together with the moored *Wellington*, *Chrysanthemum* and *President*, the latter two being RNVR training ships. The former sloop *Wellington* was acquired in 1947 by the Master Mariners' Company (formed in 1932, the first new one for over two centuries), which is unique in having a floating livery 'hall'. Behind the

trees are the Inns of Court, stretching between the Embankment and Fleet Street. The building with the tall hipped roof on the far right in front of St Paul's is the former City of London School, built 1881-2, which moved to a new site on the other side of Blackfriars Bridge in 1986. Old boys include Arthur Rackham, Dennis Norden and Mike Brearley. In 1997 *Chrysanthemum* is missing, but a sightseeing boat fills the gap. *Frank Hornby/WA*

This page The original **SOUTHWARK BRIDGE** was designed by Rennie, but was replaced in 1912-21 by the present five-span steel bridge on granite piers. This photograph, taken circa 1958, shows the buildings in Queen Street Place to good effect, the one beside the bridge being Vintry House (1927) and beyond it Thames House (1911). The site opposite has been cleared, allowing a view of the church of St Michael Paternoster Royal flanked by buildings brand new in 1958; behind them on the skyline is part of Bucklersbury House of the same year (see also pages 70-1). On the riverside, building work is in progress for Malvern House, on Queen Street Place, completed in 1961, and to its right the Corporation of London Public Cleansing Department buildings, completed in the following year.

Most of the buildings have changed by 1997. On the left, on the far side of Southwark Bridge, Vintry House has been replaced by the very attractive Vintners Place, headquarters of the Vintners Company, a modern building completed in 1992 but presenting a magnificent classical frontage to the river. Malvern House has come and gone in the intervening three and a half decades, replaced by a modern building known simply as 10 Queen Street Place. Next door is still the Cleansing Department, but today the premises are equipped with a hoist for lifting containers of refuse into barges moored alongside for shipment down river. A pleasant riverside walk, known as Three Cranes Walk, forms part of the Thames Path, and passes through the Cleansing Department premises, where it is known as Steelyard Passage and Walbrook Walk (near this spot is where the ancient Walbrook

stream - see pages 66-7 - issues into the Thames). The path will need to be closed for a maximum of 15 minutes each time a refuse container passes overhead! On the extreme right is the slim Ocean House, in Cousin Lane hard against Cannon Street railway bridge. The completed Bucklersbury House still provides the skyline. *R. C. Riley/WA*

Opposite page Swinging the camera round to look downstream, we now see **CANNON STREET RAILWAY BRIDGE**. Victorian author Samuel Butler wrote: 'When I think of . . . the huge wide-opened jaws of those two Behemoths, the Cannon Street and Charing Cross railway stations, I am not sure that the prospect

here is not even finer than in Fleet Street. See how they belch forth puffing trains as the breath of their nostrils, gorging and disgorging incessantly those human atoms whose movement is the life of the city!'

Indeed, like Charing Cross, Cannon Street did once have a vast graceful arched roof that terminated in two arcaded towers over 100 feet high, containing water tanks to power the hydraulic lifts connecting the station with the vaults below at street level. Unfortunately this roof was damaged by bombing on the night of 11-12 May 1941, rendering it unsafe for reglazing. However, it survived in skeleton form, as seen in this view of 31 May 1956, until it was dismantled in 1958, leaving the walls and towers looking

rather 'lost'. In the 1960s the station was extensively remodelled, with a 15-storey office block built across the Cannon Street end. There were plans for a flat roof over the platforms for a car park or heliport, but as can be seen in the 1996 view, office buildings, as at Charing Cross, have been built across the tracks between the towers, which survived the 1960s work through the efforts of the President of the Royal Academy and others. The offices are occupied by the London International Financial Futures & Options Exchange (LIFFE), the largest such institution outside the USA, while under the station at street level is Cannons, a fully equipped sports club.

The bridge itself is 706 feet long and was originally supported

on piers each comprising four cast iron cylinders; in 1892 it was widened on the upstream side and two further columns added. Unlike at Charing Cross, there were no high girders above rail level, making the structure much less obtrusive. The station has been electrified since 1926, and steam-hauled trains ceased to run altogether in June 1958. Having always been a principally commuter station, Cannon Street is currently only open during rush hours.

In the background in 1956 can be seen considerable bomb damage, surmounted by the Monument. On the right is the bulk of Adelaide House and New Fresh Wharf beside London Bridge, which we shall be visiting shortly. Today the wartime gaps have been filled with the plain white Mondial House, occupied by BT and incorporating a fire station on Upper Thames Street, and beyond it Ebbgate House and Seal House, replacing a 1960s multi-storey car park. *R. C. Riley/WA*

This page During the 1st century AD the Thames formed a vital defence for the native people against the Romans invading from the south, and it is certain that an early ancestor of **LONDON BRIDGE** was built by Caesar in about AD 43, about 200 feet downstream of the present one; there may have been an even earlier one. Space dictates that we must skim over the next 1,700 years or so of the history of this crucial London landmark, except to say that during that time the various bridges on this site were the only ones across the Thames in London until Putney Bridge was opened in the 1720s, then Westminster Bridge in 1750.

The last but one London Bridge was of five stone arches designed by John Rennie and built in 1823-31. The arches, of up to 152 feet span, were quite ambitious, but rested on troublesome timber foundations; widened to 65 feet in 1903-4 by cantilevering the footpaths, at the time of the Second World War it was said that more than 110,000 pedestrians and 20,000 vehicles crossed it each day.

As the accompanying photographs show, the bridge was completely rebuilt in 1967-72. The first view shows a sign describing the works, then the next two show the old and new side by side. The granite facework of the old bridge was sold to an American oil tycoon for £1 million, shipped to the US and re-erected at Lake Havasu City, Arizona. One fragment remains in situ, however, the single span across Tooley Street on the south side, 'the joints of paper-thin precision' (Pevsner). *Arthur Davenport (2)/A. J. Pike, courtesy Frank Hornby*

Opposite page On Saturday 7 October 1967 the old bridge is seen before rebuilding began. On the left on the far side of the

bridge is Fishmongers' Hall, headquarters of the City livery company of that name; it was built in 1834 with the approach roads to the new bridge. Above it is the tower of the then headquarters of the National Westminster Bank of 1962-5 with its distinctive convex back and front and inverted sides. The building on the right of the bridge is the somewhat Egyptian-looking Adelaide House of 1924-5, an early non-classical London office building (Adelaide was William IV's Queen, and they opened the new bridge in 1831).

Some 18 months later the scene has been transformed. On 28 May 1969 a vast gantry has been erected over the upstream side of the bridge, while traffic uses the other half. Note in the background the new 320-foot Stock Exchange building under construction, completed in that year. The new bridge was of three concrete cantilevered spans, on concrete piers dug deep into the clay. By early 1970 the gantry had been moved to the right and traffic to the left, and by 1971 the outer parts of the new bridge were in place and the gantry worked in the middle. By the autumn of 1972 the finishing touches were being made, and the new bridge was opened by the Queen on 16 March 1973.

The 1996 view is taken from a slightly different viewpoint, the previous pedestrian walkway having since been removed. It can be seen how much wider the new bridge is. The National Westminster Tower of 1980 has appeared on the skyline above Adelaide House, while the curved, barrel-like roof of Barclay's Bank headquarters in Lombard Street, begun in 1991, can just be seen in between. The building on the extreme right is No 1 London Bridge (1986), headquarters of Price Waterhouse.
Arthur Davenport (2)/WA

When the 19th-century German poet and essayist Heinrich Heine visited London he saw 'the greatest wonder which the world can show to the astonished spirit. I have seen it, and am more astonished than ever - and still there remains in my memory that stone forest of houses, and amid them the rushing stream of faces, of living human faces, with all their motley passions. . .' Nowhere is the 'rushing stream' more characteristic of London than the daily tide of humanity that ebbs and flows across **LONDON BRIDGE** from the railway station to the City. This wonderfully atmospheric and austere Monday morning rush hour scene of 12 July 1947 shows the old bridge and a great many hats and overcoats, a few tightly rolled umbrellas, some buses and a couple of bicycles - no private cars. At about that time it was estimated that the night population of the City was about 11,000, but that over a million people entered it during a working day, and some 436,000 worked there. By the 1980s the resident population was down to less than 6,000, with some 360,000 workers, of whom three-quarters were office workers who travelled in each day.

How different it is almost 50 years later - and yet how similar. Still the pavements are packed with commuters flooding into the City, but the traffic is far more congested and varied, and there are virtually no hats and overcoats to be seen! *London Transport Museum/WA*

Across the river in the photograph opposite can be seen **HAY'S WHARF**, featured in this closer view taken from the south side of London Bridge. This is London's oldest and largest wharf, dating from the 1650s (it is also included amongst the colour photographs). This late 1940s photograph shows that there is still a great deal of shipping being handled on what poet John Masefield described as 'The great street paved with water, filled with shipping, And all the world's flags flying and seagulls dipping.'

Following the Second World War, however, dockside activity so far up river declined, falling victim to the growth of containerisation, the need for deeper water for larger vessels, and the desire for quicker turn-rounds. Container ships are now dealt with quickly and mechanically at the Port of London's improved Tilbury Docks down river, which retain for London the title of Britain's biggest port, handling some 45 million tons of cargo annually. The former West India and Millwall Docks on the Isle of Dogs, closed in 1980, have been famously redeveloped around the Canary Wharf tower. St Katherine's Dock, immediately west of Tower Bridge and in the far left background of this 'past' view, closed in 1968 and has become housing, shops, offices and a marina; the complex's 808-bedroom Tower Thistle Hotel, opened in 1973, is the modern 'stepped' building adjacent to Tower Bridge. Hay's Wharf, meanwhile, has become a pleasant riverside walk leading down towards fashionable Hay's Galleria, an arcade of shops, bars and market stalls, outside which is moored the only representative of shipping present today apart from the modern ferry and pleasure boat pier. This is HMS *Belfast* of 1939, which has been on the Thames and open to the public since 1971. *Arthur Davenport/WA*

LONDON BRIDGE AND TOWER OF LONDON   No. 96.

NEW FRESH WHARF, adjacent to London Bridge on the north bank, is also featured amongst the colour photographs, but is included here again together with an Edwardian postcard showing the original wharves and the relative narrowness of the old bridge in the foreground, and giving some idea of the amount of shipping that once used this part of the Upper Pool.

In the second view, dating from the late 1960s, work has begun on preparations for the rebuilding of London Bridge. The taller of the buildings on the skyline is 20 Fenchurch Street, built for Kleinwort Benson in 1963-8, 'an overpowering but undeniably impressive 20-storey slab of sheer curtain-walling' (Pevsner). Beyond it is the square dark block of 6-8 Bishopsgate.

The 'present' picture shows Adelaide House again on the left, now cleaned. The demolition of the wharf warehouse has allowed a glimpse of Wren's St Magnus church, tucked in behind Adelaide House, and the two modern buildings are St Magnus House (1980) and Montague House (1986). The background skyscrapers have been joined by the National Westminster Tower on the left and, to the right of it, 168 Fenchurch Street, built for Barclays Bank in the early 1970s; in 1996 this is empty and scheduled for demolition and replacement! The wharf no longer sees any shipping, but a modern pleasure cruiser stands in for the older one in the previous photograph. *Authors' collection/A. J. Pike, courtesy of Frank Hornby/WA*

Looking a little more directly downstream, the turrets of the Tower of London can be seen in the distance. The building next to New Fresh Wharf in this 12 December 1972 photograph is **BILLINGSGATE FISH MARKET** in Lower Thames Street. Originally there were two principal wharves for fishing vessels, but that at Queenhithe was above London Bridge and sailors preferred not to have to negotiate the difficult waters between the bridge's piers. The market dated from the 11th century, but the building seen here was built in 1874-77. As soon as the 1880s is was being declared inadequate, but it was not until 1982 that it closed and moved to a new site downstream on the Isle of Dogs. The 1940 Red Guide describes it as a 'somewhat unsavoury locality . . . seen at is best (or worst) . . . short-

ly after the opening at 5 am'. Before the war between 700 and 1,100 tons of fish were being delivered to the market by 4 am. As well as the all-pervading odour of fish, Billingsgate was also a byword for foul language - in the 17th century this was referred to as 'stupendous obscenity, nitrous verbosity, and malicious scurrility'!

The large white building beyond, with a river frontage nearly 500 feet long, is the Custom House, again of ancient origin although the present building dates from the 1820s. Above it rises Bowring Tower of 1962-5 in Byward Street (see also page 59). Between there and Tower Pier the cranes and warehouses have once again been replaced by modern office development (see page 56). *Arthur Davenport/WA*

In 1994 **TOWER BRIDGE** celebrated its centenary, having been opened amidst great pomp and ceremony by the Prince of Wales (later King Edward VII) and opened to traffic on 30 June 1894; he had laid the foundation stone in 1881. Its cost was met from an ancient trust fund dating from the 12th century; this continues to pay for its upkeep, and is administered by the Corporation of London, which still owns and manages the bridge.

The apparently stone towers are in fact steel-framed and only stone faced, to take the weight of the 'bascules', the counter-weights within the piers that balance the lifting parts (*bascule* is French for 'see-saw'). The towers also contain lifts taking pedestrians to the two upper footbridges; these were provided in the expectation that the bridge would be open for long periods, but when this proved not to be the case they were closed in 1910. The stipulation for the bridge was that it must have a 135-foot head-

room and a clear width of 200 feet. The 270-foot approach spans were built on the suspension principle, and the bridge had a hydraulic mechanism until electrified in 1976.

The 1940 Red Guide says: 'A bell is rung when the "elevation" is about to take place, which happens about fourteen times daily. . . [in the 1990s the average was down to about 500 times a year]. About 5,000 vehicles and more than four times that number of pedestrians use the bridge daily. . .' (In 1995 a traffic census saw almost 35,000 vehicles in Tower Bridge Road during a 24-hour period.) In those days a tug was kept permanently in steam to assist vessels who might get into difficulty - this facility, part of the conditions for the building of the bridge, cost nearly £3,000 annually, but was hardly ever used. Perhaps it is the tug in the foreground of this superb composite photograph dated 10 May 1956. It also shows the extent of the docks on both sides of the river, now all gone; those on the south (right) bank were known as Butlers Wharf, now providing office, residential and retail accommodation, including the Conran Gastrodome restaurant.

Note the children playing on the 'beach' on the left. The Red Guide announces that 'the adjacent stretch of sand is one of the many "Children's Lidos" constructed in recent years.' Even today, with the Thames as clean as at any time in the last 200 years, this activity is not encouraged!

Tower Bridge has now been cleaned and returned to all its Victorian Gothic glory, and on the left-hand pier can be seen the entrance to 'The Tower Bridge Experience', one of London's leading tourist attractions complete with animatronic figures, lasers and interactive displays; since 1982 the footbridges have also been open again. Note the open-top tourist bus crossing the centre of the bridge. *C. F. B. Penley, A. Mott collection/WA*

This superb view of the southern approach to **TOWER BRIDGE**, dated Thursday 12 September 1946, reminds us of the huge changes in daily life that have taken place over the ensuing half-century! On the left an open horse-drawn wagon is being overtaken by a canvas-topped lorry; there are at least two other horse-drawn vehicles on the bridge. Note also the superb J. Lyons lorry and trailer, presumably returning empty, tarpaulins rolled, to a depot, the diminutive Austin 7 parked on the right, and the gas-lamps.

The only building to survive in 1996, apart from the now con-spicuously clean bridge itself, is the one on the left, which houses the Tower Bridge Engineer and Bridge Master's Office. Below the approach on the left, where Tower Bridge Wharf once stood, is now the Tower Bridge Park. It's a Bank Holiday, so parking is more rife than on a normal weekday, but traffic is still heavy. In the distance, just to the right of the 17-ton weight restriction sign, is the tower of the former Trinity Square headquarters of the Port of London Authority, built in 1912-22. Sold in 1971 as the docks began to close, the PLA is now based at St Katharine's Dock. *London Transport Museum/WA*

We are now standing on **TOWER BRIDGE** looking upstream back towards the Custom House and Billingsgate on the far bank, in a scene full of activity taken on Sunday 25 September 1955. The 'flatiron' collier *Adams Beck* is heading downstream, apparently empty, through the bridge, while on the right an RAF Sunderland flying-boat is moored. In the left middle distance is Tower Pier, with pleasure craft large and small. On the horizon at the far left is the Monument, then a little further right the slender spire of Wren's St Dunstan-in-the-East.

By 1997 the rest of the 1955 buildings in the City have been largely replaced, or at least overpowered by modern building. Behind Tower Pier the conspicuous light-coloured block was built as the offices of the General Steam Navigation Co in 1956-60 and in 1996 is awaiting a new tenant. Beyond, the modern block is Sugar Quay, containing flats and Tate & Lyle's offices; the old wooden quay itself is fenced off as unsafe. Above Sugar Quay are Bowring Tower and 20 Fenchurch Street, then, rising above the trees surrounding the Tower of London, Minster Court, its dramatic gabled roof-line, like some medieval Gothic cathedral, enhancing the view far more than its more 'slabby' neighbours. Built in 1986-90 on a 4-acre site, this £400 million development is actually three buildings, one occupied by the London Underwriting Centre, the others by Prudential Assurance. Incidentally, Minster Court had a small part in Disney's 1996 live-action *101 Dalmatians* as 'The House of De Vil', Cruella's fashion business! Behind rises once again the mass of the National Westminster Tower, and to the right the dark mass of 6-8 Bishopsgate. Not as bulky as *Adams Beck*, but still a craft of considerable size, the appropriately named *Millennium of London* passes upstream. *Frank Hornby/WA*

This view from Tower Stairs, near **TOWER PIER**, was taken on the previous day, 24 September 1955. Bankside Power Station's chimney can be seen on the horizon above the old London Bridge and the wharfside cranes on the south bank. A freighter is moored at Sugar Quay, its warehouses shortly to give way to General Steam Navigation's new building, while in the foreground a group sun themselves on the deck of their cabin cruiser, with rowing-boats tied alongside. Note the British Road Services eight-wheeler parked on the quay.

The 1996 view is partly obscured by modern access to today's Tower Pier, but vestiges of the old wharf can been seen just right of centre. From here before the war, the Red Guide tells us, 'pleasure steamers leave on day trips to Southend, Margate, etc. Other steamers and also motor launches ply to and from Greenwich and Westminster.' Today boats still leave for Greenwich and Westminster and other short-cruise destinations. Bankside's chimney can still be seen above the modern development around Southwark Bridge, while No 1 London Bridge dominates the extreme left of the view. The slender new London Bridge completes the scene. *Frank Hornby/WA*

4. THE CITY

The **TOWER OF LONDON** is almost 900 years old, so one would not expect there to have been much change during the last 50! Of course its role as a tourist attraction has seen many developments, and it is there that the biggest changes have occurred. This view from Tower Hill is looking at the western side of the fortress. The modern-day ticket office is off the picture to the right, and today a taxi rank and narrow single-lane one-way car and coach access road are clearly delineated by bollards, where in the 1950s there was just an expanse of cobbled roadway. The benches, litter-bins, road salt bunker and 'Doctor Who' police box have all gone, to be replaced by two modern telephone kiosks. Clearly the tree on the left is the same one, although the others seem to be different. Both photographs were taken from an elevated paved area, under which today is a subterranean Macdonald's restaurant and the Tower Hill Pageant.

Of the Tower itself, on the right is Beauchamp Tower, on the left St Stephen's Chapel, with the bulk of the central keep, the White Tower, in the centre. In 1914 the Tower was open on Saturdays, Mondays and public holidays, and admission was free except on public holidays, when it was 6d or 1 shilling, depending on the parts viewed. In the early 1940s admission to the whole site was 1s 3d, and some parts were still free on Saturdays and Bank Holidays. Today the Tower is No 5 in the ranking of London attractions, with over 2.3 million visitors in 1993 (the other four are the British Museum, National Gallery, Westminster Abbey and Madame Tussauds); in 1996 the entrance charge was £8.30 per adult (with concessions) and £5.50 for children, and the area is thronged with queuing tourists, indicating the increased importance of the international leisure industry today and the amount being spent by the visitors! *C. F. B. Penley, A. Mott collection/WA*

THE PRESENT COAL EXCHANGE.

A few hundred yards west of the Tower, in **LOWER THAMES STREET**, was the Coal Exchange, one of the earliest cast-iron buildings in London and the best in England, according to Pevsner. It was opened in 1849, Roman remains having been discovered when its foundations were dug. The rotunda had a glass roof and very elaborate cast-iron galleries on three floors; its floor was made of black oak from the Tyne inlaid with 4,000 pieces of wood shaped to represent a mariner's compass. A wind dial helped the coal dealers calculate the likely time of arrival of shipments up the river.

In the early 1960s the City Corporation proposed a new dual carriageway road along the route of Lower and Upper Thames Street to link the Tower with Blackfriars and the Victoria Embankment. Amongst other things this required the doubling of the width of the road bridge beneath Cannon Street station, which was completed in June 1964. It also necessitated the demolition of one side of Lower Thames Street, which, as can be seen from the 'past' photograph dated 3 June 1962, was only a relatively narrow side street (the lamps and canopies on the rear of Billingsgate Fish Market are visible on the extreme right, where the Ford Thames lorry - appropriately enough! - is parked). There was much controversy about whether the south or north side should go, since the rear of the Custom House was unremarkable while the Coal Exchange was the opposite; however, it was decided on the north side, and amid protests the Exchange was pulled down in 1962 ('tragedy by stupidity' is Pevsner's verdict).

Today the new Lower Thames Street sweeps down from Tower Hill past Bowring Tower of 1962-5 in Byward Street. Billingsgate still stands on the right, and the street on the corner of which the Coal Exchange stood (St Mary at Hill) emerges between the older buildings and the new office block (St Mary's Court) on the left; the Exchange would have been approximately where the central reservation is today. *Authors' collection/R. C. Riley/WA*

We are now looking up Monument Street towards Christopher Wren's **MONUMENT**, built in 1671-7 for the Corporation of London (who still maintain it today) to commemorate the Great Fire of London of 2-6 September 1666; as the authorising Act put it, 'to preserve the memory of this dreadful Visitation', a 'Column or Pillar' was to be 'erected on or as neere unto the place where the said Fire soe unhappily began. . .' The fire actually began in Pudding Lane, 202 feet away from the base of the tower, which is itself 202 feet high. Made of Portland stone, it contains 311 steps, and it is the tallest isolated stone column in the world. It is surmounted by a gilt bronze flaming urn, symbolising the fire.

The first view (*below*) shows Monument Street and the tower on 4 May 1960; note the suspended gas-lamp, and the three-wheel Scammell 'mechanical horse' dray at the top of the street. Consequent upon the development of Lower Thames Street, the lower part of Monument Street was redeveloped. The second view (*right*), dated 7 October 1978, shows that the south side of the street has been demolished for 'new office development'. On the right-hand side at the top, Faryners House of 1971 is new, but the older buildings, including the 'Billingsgate Christian Mission', survive, available for refurbishment.

Today's view shows the dramatic modern building, the slender Peninsula House, that now occupies the corner of Monument Street and the new dual-carriageway Lower Thames Street. The buildings on the right are again available for sale or let. *Arthur Davenport/Frank Hornby/WA*

'From here the view is magnificent,' wrote Arthur Mee in 1937, 'the Thames winding to the sea between the wharves and docks and the spires of the City churches.' Some 175 years earlier, in 1762, Dr Johnson's companion James Boswell had climbed to the top, but found it 'horrid to be so monstrous a way up in the air, so far above London and all its spires.' Six suicides between 1788 and 1842 led to the gallery being encased in an iron cage, which your authors can confirm instils a greater feeling of security at such a height than might otherwise be the case. . .!

The Blitz of 1940-41 was to change that City panorama for ever. The total area devastated was roughly the same as that razed by the Great Fire, but led to massive replanning on a scale undreamed of even by Wren. The City would have to be largely rebuilt from the gas and water mains upwards, and while many of the famous spires were to survive, their

churches were often gutted or destroyed. The process of redevelopment is still very much under way today.

Close examination of this **VIEW FROM THE MONUMENT**, taken on Monday 25 April 1955, shows many bomb sites and partly destroyed buildings. In the bottom right-hand corner is the roof of Billingsgate Fish Market, with Britannia astride the central pediment. Next door is the great Custom House, and in front of it Custom House Quay. Running along behind it is the pre-widening Lower Thames Street, and the remarkable glass roof and corner turret of the Coal Exchange can be clearly seen. The slender spire on the left is that of St Dunstan-in-the-East. Originally built in the 13th century, it largely survived the Great Fire, although the tower had to be rebuilt. It is said that Wren's daughter had a hand in the design of the four graceful flying buttresses supporting the lantern and spire. The rest of the church was rebuilt in 1817, then destroyed in the Blitz. In 1971 what remained was restored and turned into a garden. In the left middle distance can be seen Tower Hill and the Tower itself, from an angle similar to the photographs on page 58. Beyond are the smoky-grey warehouses of St Katherine's Dock, then to the right Tower Bridge and yet more wharves and cranes.

Today's view is very different. As we have seen, Lower Thames Street has been made into a east-west through route, and St Mary's Court now occupies the site of the Coal Exchange, while Billingsgate is almost obscured by Peninsula House on the right. The Tower is behind Bowring Tower on Byward Street, and the St Katherine's Dock warehouses have been replaced by the Tower Thistle Hotel. Tower Bridge gleams in its newfound cleanliness, and on the extreme right the warehouses have given way to Tower Bridge Park; the stern of HMS *Belfast* can also be seen. *Arthur Davenport/WA*

Opposite page This is **BANK**, right at the beating heart of the City! On the left is 'the old lady of Threadneedle Street' herself, the Bank of England, founded in 1694 to lend money to the Government. The building dates from 1732, and the whole of the 3½-acre site was finished by the end of the 1780s. Then in 1921-37 it was entirely rebuilt, except for the lower outer 'screen wall' seen here, a loss bemoaned by Pevsner as 'the worst individual loss suffered by London architecture in the first half of the 20th century'. The Bank of England was nationalised by the Attlee Government in 1946, and has seen its role continually evolving as the commercial and international life of the nation has evolved since the war. The building on the right with the massive portico is the Royal Exchange, of which more in a moment.

The past view is dated Saturday 30 May 1953, and all the buildings are decorated to mark the Coronation of Queen Elizabeth II the following Tuesday. A taxi is leaving Threadneedle Street (originally Threeneedle Street, from the arms of the Needlemakers, possibly the sign of a nearby tavern), while an *Evening News* van waits to turn; this newspaper was published in London from 1881 until it was merged with the *Evening Standard* in 1980; its last edition went on sale on Friday 31 October. David English, then editor of the *Daily Mail*, said, 'It caught the flavour of London in a way unmatched by any of its rivals.'

Although today's traffic lights are no doubt more sophisticated than those in 1953, traffic control at Bank is still done with the minimum of road markings and a similar number of 'Keep Left' bollards; it is clearly still left to drivers to navigate this busiest of junctions by common sense. . . Glowering over the scene in 1996 is the new 320-foot-high Stock Exchange building completed in 1969, and behind it the ever-present National Westminster Tower. The Duke of Wellington on horseback oversees matters from his plinth outside the Royal Exchange. *Arthur Davenport/WA*

This page Still dominating the background of this second view of **BANK** is the Royal Exchange. Founded in the 16th century by financier Thomas Gresham as a rival for the *bourse* in Antwerp, the original building was a victim of the Great Fire. Its replacement also burned down, in 1838, and the present building, the third, was opened by Queen Victoria in 1844; the central figure in the pediment is Commerce. It ceased its original function in 1939, but is still occupied by Guardian Royal Exchange Assurance. On the right is the domed No 1 Cornhill, built in 1905 for the former Liverpool & London & Globe Insurance Company, whose name is still on the building in the 'past' view, of unknown date (although as a clue the 76 bus is advertising the *Star* newspaper with 'Attlee's Own Story' - he was PM 1945-51, then Leader of the Opposition until his resignation in 1955). On the right are the columns of the Mansion House.

The cleanliness of the buildings and more up-to-date traffic and pedestrian control are almost the only differences between these two views. Swinging into Queen Victoria Street is a Mercedes, the modern luxury equivalent of the handsome car (a Jaguar?) seen in the 'past' picture. *London Transport Museum/WA*

We are now standing on the steps of the Royal Exchange looking west across the **BANK** junction on Wednesday 6 May 1959. Let the Red Guide of 1940 describe the scene: '. . .although "the Bank" originally implied solely the Bank of England, the neighbourhood is now so closely packed with British and foreign banks and financial organisation as to merit the designation "The Bank of the World". . . Both above and below ground this is a busy spot . . . here converge no fewer than seven of the most important thoroughfares, each filled from morn till night with an unending stream of omnibuses, motors, lorries, cyclists and pedestrians. A recent official count gave an average at the Bank of over 3,000 vehicles an hour; while underground over 600 trains a day bring people to or from this busy centre. . . Until the installation of control lights at all important road crossings and junctions a large proportion of the City police force were engaged in the regulation of traffic, and many still are so.

'Dexterity of no common order is required to get across the roadways in safety, and pedestrians, especially strangers, are strongly advised to make use of the circular Subway from which short stairways give access to all the diverging thoroughfares.'

On the left is the entrance to one of these subways, which also serves Bank station, opened by the then City & South London Railway (now part of the Northern Line) in February 1900. The booking hall was built in the crypt of an 18th-century church, costing the company £170,000 in compensation; the contractor was Mowlem, who went on to build the new London Bridge 70 years later. The section of the Northern Line from East Finchley to Morden via Bank forms the longest continual tunnel in the world - 17 miles 528 yards. Bank is also on the Waterloo & City tube line, a curiosity linking it with Waterloo station and owned by successive main-line railway companies; held in scant affection by its patrons, it is known as 'The Drain'.

Incidentally, the *Star*'s hoarding beside the subway entrance announces

'Marwood Decision - Butler Speaks'. Ronald Marwood had stabbed a policeman during a brawl outside an Islington nightclub in December 1958. He had been found guilty, and on 2 May petitions had been received by the then Home Secretary, R. A. Butler, for a reprieve. This was refused on the 7th, and despite demonstrations and further petitions on the 8th, Marwood was hanged on the following day.

In the middle distance is the statue of Wellington, while in the right foreground is a memorial to London troops of both World Wars. On the right is the Bank of England, and beyond, on the corner of Princes Street and Poultry, the great mass of the National Westminster Bank, begun in 1929 and recently refurbished; echoes of the past are everywhere, for a Neolithic stone axe was found on the site. Straight ahead, on the corner of Poultry and Queen Victoria Street is the turreted No 1 Poultry of 1875. On the extreme left is the Mansion House, the official residence of the Lord Mayor of London during his year of office. Completed in 1752 at a cost of more than £70,000, it was damaged during the war, repairs lasting until 1950. Here work the holders of such ancient offices as Swordbearer, Common Cryer, Serjeant-at-Arms and City Marshal, who attend the Lord Mayor on state occasions.

The Neolithic stone axe reminds us that, like some great forest, the City of London, indeed London as a whole, is continually renewing itself, season by season, century upon century, layer upon layer. In 1997 No 1 Poultry is swathed in plastic, the 1875 building being replaced by a startling modern design, as seen on the hoarding attached to the works (*above*). Planning permission was granted in 1989, just before a ruling was made obliging developers to pay for archaeological digs on sites such as this. However, the developers and English Heritage agreed to provide £2 million for an excavation, which was to become one of London's most valuable archaeological explorations.

Before the Victorian buildings were demolished, trial trenches were sunk 3 to 5 metres into the land that 2,000 years earlier had been the marshy banks of the Walbrook stream, on the low hills beside which the Romans built their city. The existence of remarkable remains was confirmed, and a bronze Roman lamp, complete with hanging chains and hook, and a crescent-shaped spacer to hold it away from the wall, was unearthed.

Meanwhile the massive piles of the new building were sunk deep into the earth and a huge concrete slab built upon them to form the base of the new development. Beneath it, in a subterranean area of some 10,000 square metres, the archaeologists worked on in artificial light and pumped-in fresh air. Down they dug through the centuries to AD 50, to the beautifully preserved oak piles of a Roman building (whose growth rings will enable its accurate dating, perhaps destroyed at the time of Queen Boadicea's revolt in AD 60), a 2nd century AD 4-metre-square mosaic, and 4th-century pottery. Trodden into the floors were fragments of broken pottery and coins, while the drainage channels yielded animal and fish bones and plant seeds. Also found was a pair of tiny scales with two cups, perhaps used by a shopkeeper, possibly Roman, possibly Saxon.

Then there is silence. From the mid-5th century to the 10th century there is nothing, as if the site lay unoccupied for 500 years. 'There are no fires, no coins, no dropped trinkets, nothing,' says Museum of London project manager Peter Rowsome. 'It just stops.'

Then in the 10th century a cattle market was established on the site, succeeded much later by the poultry market that gave the street its name. In the 11th century a church was built there, with a burial ground used until the church was destroyed in the Great Fire. The Roman Watling Street is nearby, and the medieval street of Bucklersbury cuts through the site.

Some 10,000 cubic metres of material will have been lifted through 'moling holes' in the concrete slab by the time the excavation is complete, and between 25,000 and 50,000 drawings will have been produced. But the basements of the new building will go down four floors, so nothing can be left in situ. It is an awesome once-only opportunity to open a window on 2,000 years of London's history, and English Heritage and the site's developers are to be congratulated on their foresight in allowing the excavation.

And so we emerge blinking into the daylight, and the noise and traffic fumes of the Bank in March 1997, with a greater sense of the almost unimaginable vastness of human history that lies literally a few feet below the pavement. *Arthur Davenport/WA (3)*

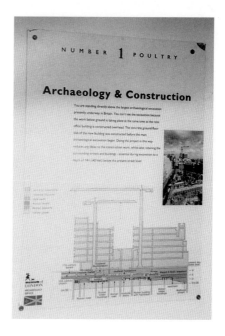

Another of the City's ancient sites is the **GUILDHALL**, which dates from the first half of the 15th century. At over 150 feet long it is the second largest hall in England (after Westminster Hall), and is the centre of civic government, where Lord Mayors and Sheriffs are elected and the Court of Common Council, the effective governing body of the City, meets. In the past important trials were also held here, and it is the venue for the annual Lord Mayor's banquet.

In December 1940 the Guildhall was set alight by bombs, and although the roof collapsed the medieval portions of the building, which had been much altered over the years, survived. A temporary steel roof was used until 1953, when a new one, covered in Collyweston stone tiles, was designed by Sir Giles Gilbert Scott. The frontage dates from 1788-9, part classical, part Gothic, its fluted buttresses topped with what Pevsner calls 'Greek bits and pieces'.

The 28 January 1968 view shows, in Arthur Mee's words, 'its great white front . . . at the end of a deep courtyard, a charming spectacle, with the Art Gallery on the right and the Magistrates Court on the left.' These rather gloomy flanking buildings have since been demolished, producing a pleasant wide open square, on the west side of which is the new wing of 1969-74 by Sir Giles Scott Son & Partners (*below*), which contains the Guildhall Library, offices, committee rooms and the Aldermen's court room. *Frank Hornby/WA (2)*

There's an air of post-war austerity about this view of **ST PAUL'S CATHEDRAL**, taken in the mid-1950s. The image of the dome standing proud amidst the conflagration of the Blitz is well known, and as can be seen here a great deal of bomb damage surrounded it. Its predecessor had not been so lucky in the Great Fire of 1666, and was replaced by what is believed to be the fourth cathedral on this site, Wren's masterpiece, built between 1675 and 1710.

The empty bombsite on the left has been filled with Bracken House (built in 1956-9 for the *Financial Times* and refurbished in 1991), just visible on the left on the corner of Friday Street. The slightly earlier building opposite is Gateway House, just completed when the 'past' photograph was taken. In front of it, in what is now a leafy garden, is the also brand new City of London Information Pavilion, which survives today on a different site a 100 yards or so down St Paul's Churchyard (*bottom*).

The small church immediately next to

it, overshadowed by St Paul's, is St Augustine Watling Street, also by Wren. Its lead spire and most of the church were destroyed in the war, but as can be seen in the 1996 view a replica of the spire has since been replaced, and the tower is now part of the new St Paul's Choir School built behind it in the 1960s. The building next to it has gone, and the whole area along the south side of the cathedral is now pleasant gardens and a coach park. Cannon Street (foreground) and Friday Street are part of a one-way system, which in May 1996 was blocked by a police check-point in the wake of the various City terrorist bomb outrages. *N. L. Browne, courtesy Frank Hornby/WA (2)*

On your behalf we wound our way up the 375 steps to the Stone Gallery around the base of the dome of **ST PAUL'S CATHEDRAL** to take the present-day equivalents of this series of 'past' aerial views taken on a sunny Thursday 17 September 1959. The gallery is over 300 feet above street level, while the cross on the top of the dome is a dizzying 365 feet.

The first view is looking eastwards towards the Monument - it is in a sense one step further back from the view on pages 62-3. We are looking along Cannon Street, while Queen Victoria Street, cut diagonally through the City in 1867-71 (with the District Line running beneath it) to link it with Blackfriars, runs middle right to top left through the centre of the picture.

In the left foreground can be seen the very top of St Augustine's tower, now with its spire restored. Beyond that is Gateway House, already seen on the previous page (the Information Pavilion has already been removed from its garden, nowadays pleasantly leafy), then the slender tower of St Mary Aldermary, completed after the Fire in 1704; John Milton married his third wife in the pre-Fire church in 1663. Beyond again is the great slab of Bucklersbury House (1953-8), a 14-storey, 204-feet-high block running between Queen Victoria Street and Cannon Street, one of the largest London office developments of the 1950s. Today, of course, even taller blocks stand behind it.

In the distance in 1959 can be seen (left to right) the Monument, Tower Bridge and, in the picture.

front of it, the bulk of Adelaide House, London Bridge. In front of that, running across the picture, are the roofless side-walls of Cannon Street station with its twin towers at the river end (the remains of the bomb-damaged roof having been removed the previous year). Today a modern office development covers a large part of the station, and at the Cannon Street end is Bush Lane House of 1976, with its distinctive external lattice-work of tubular stainless steel.

In front of the station walls can be seen the tower of St Michael Paternoster Royal, completed in 1713, one of Wren's last, and further to the right St James Garlickhithe, also by Wren. Directly below St Michael in 1959 can be seen the ruins of St Mildred Bread Street, another of the 19 churches ruined in the Blitz and one of three to have now disappeared altogether.

Nearer the camera, the buildings on the Cannon Street/Friday Street/Queen Victoria Street triangle, including St Mildred's, being pulled down in 1959, have all been replaced. The first new building on the corner of Friday Street, put up in 1960-1, was itself pulled down and replaced in 1983 by a new 18-20 Cannon Street. Beyond, the triangular building is No 30. The recently refurbished Bracken House is in the right foreground, and in the bottom right-hand corner is Old Change House, still under construction in 1959 and apparently refaced since then. *Arthur Davenport/WA*

The camera now turns to look north, across what in 1959 was an area of considerable bomb damage, being used as a car park. This entire area, known as Paternoster Square, was developed between 1961 and 1967 from plans drawn up as early as 1956. The buildings are 6 feet above ground to allow for car parking beneath; the tallest part is the 16-storey tower on the left, mostly of glass. Laid out with shops, restaurants, cafes and flower boxes, it was hailed as one of the better examples of its kind, but unfortunately at the time of writing the entire office complex - known as Sudbury House - is empty, and the area has a sadly neglected look.

The street on the right is King Edward Street, and the ruined church on the corner is

Wren's Christ Church of 1677-8. The nave and aisles were destroyed in the war, and the tower is in course of restoration in the 1959 view. Behind it is the complex stretching almost the whole width of the picture that was once the headquarters of the General Post Office. The foundation stone was laid by King Edward VII in 1905, and the building was completed in 1911, one of the first reinforced concrete structures in Britain; it is now Royal Mail's City and International Office. It also now houses the National Postal Museum, opened in 1966. On the extreme right of the 1996 view is another building with communications connections, BT Centre, the headquarters of BT since 1984. *Arthur Davenport/WA*

Swinging round again, we are now facing approximately north-west, and the foreground today is again dominated by the Paternoster Square development, obscuring the greater part of the detail seen in the 1959 view. In the centre of both pictures is the dome of the Old Bailey, or more correctly the Central Criminal Court, built on the site of the infamous Newgate Prison; the present building was opened by King Edward VII in 1907, but severely damaged during the war. On top of the dome, 121 feet above the street, stands the famous figure of Justice, blindfolded with scales in one hand and a sword in the other. To the left in the 1996 view can be seen the 1967-72 extensions, which now provide a total of 19 court-rooms.

The church to the right of the dome is St Sepulchre, Newgate Street, another Great Fire

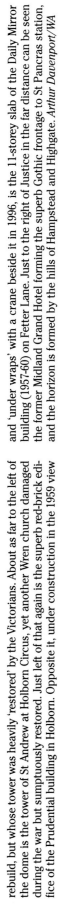

rebuild, but whose tower was heavily 'restored' by the Victorians. About as far to the left of the dome is the tower of St Andrew at Holborn Circus, yet another Wren church damaged during the war but sumptuously restored. Just left of that again is the superb red-brick edifice of the Prudential building in Holborn. Opposite it, under construction in the 1959 view and 'under wraps' with a crane beside it in 1996, is the 11-storey slab of the Daily Mirror building (1957-60) on Fetter Lane. Just to the right of Justice in the far distance can be seen the former Midland Grand Hotel forming the superb Gothic frontage to St Pancras station, and the horizon is formed by the hills of Hampstead and Highgate. *Arthur Davenport/WA*

Finally, we are now looking more or less west, up river towards Westminster. Dominating the right of the pictures is the south-west tower of the great west front of St Paul's, described by Pevsner as 'the most Baroque of all Wren's spires . . . coupled columns projecting in the diagonals and convex bays with columns between them, then complex volutes [spiral scrolls] leading up to an octagonal lantern and an ogee [double curved] cap. The whole is much more intricate than this description can convey.' Indeed, the only way to really appreciate the intricacies of Wren's architecture is to get this close.

The 1959 cityscape down towards the river is a ramshackle affair of roofs and chimneys. It is somewhat less cluttered in 1996, thanks to the development connected with the Upper Thames Street underpass; this runs beneath the modern riverward buildings, the platforms of Blackfriars station and Blackfriars Bridge, to join the Victoria Embankment in front of the curved, colonnaded building on the corner of the Embankment and New Bridge Street (Unilever House of 1930-31). In the centre of this area can be seen the tower of St Andrew-by-the-Wardrobe, another Wren church of 1685-96. Opposite, in Queen Victoria Street, the famous Mermaid Theatre was converted from a warehouse in 1959. Nearby in Tudor times was Baynard's Castle, its tall turreted front rising from the river; of Norman origin, traces were discovered in 1972-74 on the site of the new City of London School for Boys, just off the picture to the left. On the far side of the river is the massive King's Reach development of the 1970s, the river frontage dominated by the more recent Sea Containers House. Following the river round we see again landmarks already encountered in the previous section of this book: the OXO tower, South Bank Television Centre, National Theatre, Royal Festival Hall, Shell Tower, Houses of Parliament, then right round to the left of King's Reach Tower, Millbank Tower. *Arthur Davenport/WA*

5. HOLBORN AND CHARING CROSS

We continue our journey westwards by walking down Ludgate Hill from St Paul's, crossing Ludgate Circus (see the colour photographs) and entering **FLEET STREET**. Bomb damage nearer St Paul's is still evident in this June 1952 photograph, and the famous railway bridge over Ludgate Hill can just be glimpsed among the buses and other traffic. In recent years Ludgate Hill has been largely redeveloped and the bridge has gone, to be replaced by City Thameslink station beneath the road.

According to the 1940 guide-book, Fleet Street is 'famous the world over as the journalistic centre of London. In or near it are the offices of nearly all the great newspapers and periodicals, where hosts of busy toilers are at work both day and night.' Arthur Mee adds at about the same period, 'Day and night, week after week, year after year, generation after generation, Fleet Street thunders without ceasing.' In this view the 1924 premises of *The Star* and the *News Chronicle* are marked by the clock on the right, those of the *Daily Telegraph* (1928) by the clock on the left. *The Star* was London's third daily after the *Standard* and *Evening News*, and disappeared with the *News Chronicle* in 1960.

It was in January 1986 that the 'toilers' of the *Sun* and *News of the World* were told that they were to move to new offices at Wapping in Docklands. So began the migration of newspapers from Fleet Street east to Docklands or west to Kensington, and the bitter trade union demonstrations against what became known as 'Fortress Wapping'. By 1990 the *Daily Telegraph* building was closed for redevelopment, as was the famous black glass and chrome building of the *Daily Express*. Next door to Chronicle House, which survives today, is The Press Association and Reuters, who are still there in the 1990s. Nearer the camera, attractive and imaginative modern buildings give today's Fleet Street a brighter appearance.

The bus is a 'Regent Mark III', commonly known as the 'RT', thousands of which plied London streets from 1939 to 1979. They were gradually replaced by the equally well-loved 'Routemasters', built 1959-68 and still in widespread use today; two are seen passing the same spot in 1996. *London Transport Museum/WA*

We are now looking down **FARRINGDON STREET** south towards Ludgate Circus, at right-angles to Fleet Street; round the curve in the distance is Blackfriars Bridge and the Embankment. This street follows the valley of the Fleet River, or Holbourn, the other stream which, with the Walbrook, bisected ancient London. Imagine this scene at any time between the 13th and 17th century, when the foul-smelling river acted as virtually an open sewer, full of discarded butchers' carcases and other refuse, as well as the outfall of 'houses of office' standing over it! After the Great Fire the lower 700 yards were turned into a canal with wharves, but it was little used and again filled with rubbish. In the mid-18th century it was culverted and Farringdon Street created.

This July 1961 photograph shows the street full of traffic, with unrestricted parking on both sides and in the middle. Today parking metres (introduced to London with 'yellow lines' in 1958) regulate roadside parking, and the centre of the road is reserved for motor cycles. The modern building on the left was built in 1954-7 for IPC Magazines; opposite it is Fleet Building, a large telephone exchange dating from 1956-60. The building under construction by Trollope & Colls in 1962 was refurbished in 1983.

Both photographs were taken from Holborn Viaduct, a superb

cast iron bridge designed to connect Newgate Street and Holborn across the Fleet valley. It is 1,400 feet long and 80 feet wide, and was opened by Queen Victoria in 1869. Could the Bedford cattle lorry from Gravesend be heading for Smithfield meat market on the north side of the viaduct? *London Transport Museum/WA*

This page A few hundred yards west of Holborn Viaduct is Holborn Circus, then **HOLBORN** heads westwards eventually to join Oxford Street. This is the view looking east in November 1959 near the junction with Grays Inn Road. On the extreme right is a corner of the Prudential Assurance building of 1879, in fiery red brick and terracotta. The modern building beyond the corner of Grays Inn Road is Bishop's House (1955-7), surmounted by a strange open-trellis canopy, since removed. On the left of the 1996 view can be seen the 'zig-zag' frontage of National Westminster House of 1965-8, and just a glimpse of the half-timbered Staple Inn, the best surviving such building in London, albeit heavily restored; it is familiar from the packets of 'High Holborn' tobacco, sold there by John Brumfit Ltd since 1933.

The main point of interest, though, are the trolleybuses, setting off from Holborn on route 521 to North Finchley and 543 to Wood Green Station. The first trolleybuses ran in London in 1935, reaching Holborn in 1938; by 1940 there were some 1,700 of them, compared with a dwindling tram fleet of only 1,077 cars. They were quieter and more comfortable than the trams they began to replace, but were still restricted by the need for the overhead power supply, and delays were caused when the trolleys jumped the wires. The last tram ran in July 1952, and in 1954 the replace-ment of trolleybuses by diesel buses was announced; by May 1962 they had all gone.

In 1996 a trusty Routemaster passes the same spot, followed by a 'non-red' London bus of one of the independent operators following deregulation in 1984. A rear-engined bus stands on the left; by 1990 the vast majority of the capital's buses had rear or under-floor engines. The memorial in the middle of the road is to the Royal Fusiliers, City of London Regiment. Note also the surviving bollard in the foreground nearly 40 years on. *Frank Hornby/WA*

Opposite page We are now looking back towards the Grays Inn Road junction from **HIGH HOLBORN** a month or two later on 29 January 1960. The old timbered Staple Inn buildings are in the right background; towering above them is the Daily Mirror building, covered in sheeting in 1996, which we saw from St Paul's (pages 74-5). Apart from the building next door to Staple Inn, the shops and offices on the south side of the street were swept away in the mid-1960s to make way for Heron House (1967-9) with its curious bal-cony-like horizontal bands. Where its fellow, National Westminster House, now stands was in 1960 a branch of the District Bank, one of three constituents of NatWest, the others being the Westminster and National Provincial. On the left can be seen the towers of the Prudential building, hidden in 1996 by the scaffolding, while on the skyline is the ubiq-uitous National Westminster Tower!

Prominent amongst the cars are a parked Ford Prefect and another in the traffic queue; behind the former is a motor cycle delivery man carrying engraved printing blocks from Swains. The London Co-operative Society was formed in 1921 and since 1980 has been part of London Regional Co-operative Retail Services Ltd, one of London's three Co-ops. *London Transport Museum/WA*

A little further west, High Holborn is bisected by **SOUTHAMPTON ROW** from the north and Kingsway to the south. In Southampton Row, at its junction with Theobalds Road, was the northern entrance of the Kingsway tram tunnel, which linked the north and south London tram systems (there were no trams in the central area) by running southwards beneath Kingsway, the western part of Aldwych and Lancaster Place to issue out on to the Victoria Embankment alongside the old Waterloo Bridge. There were intermediate 'Tramway Stations' with 'island' platforms near Holborn and opposite Bush House, Aldwych. In *The King's England* Arthur Mee remarks that 'the tall double-decker trams dive underground to reappear on the Embankment half a mile away, an entertainment the children find as good as a switchback.'

The tunnel was opened with the new street, named in honour of King Edward VII, in 1906, and was originally for single-deckers only. This proved too restrictive, so in 1929-31 is was deepened to take double-deckers. By 1940 it formed part of one of only three remaining tram routes in north, west and east London; there had been experiments with the use of specially adapted trolleybuses, but this proved impracticable. The tunnel closed in April 1952, a couple of months before the end of the trams, and was left abandoned; in 1957 it became a store for machine parts. On 21 January 1964 the southern portion of the tunnel, between the bottom of Kingsway and Lancaster Place, re-opened as a twisting road tunnel taking traffic from Waterloo Bridge to Kingsway without the need to negotiate the Strand/Aldwych junction.

This view, taken in 1951, sees tram No 1956 breasting the climb; presumably it is stationary at the busy Theobalds Road junction, judging by the pedestrians walking in front! Note the red/green signal on the lamp standard, to prevent more than one tram at a time being on the 1 in 10 slope.

The 100-feet-wide Kingsway was the most extensive road development in central London since Regent Street had been built in 1820, and acquisition of the land cost £4½ million. The buildings in the background form the outer face of one side of the Sicilian Avenue triangle of 1905, a short but attractive shopping arcade paved with Sicilian marble, the entrance to which can be seen in the 1996 view between the turreted corners. The offices (originally flats) are clad in a mixture of bright red brick and white terracotta, and are newly cleaned. *N. L. Browne, courtesy Frank Hornby/WA*

TRAMS

No	Destination	Route
2 (See also 4)	VICTORIA EMBKT.	Via: Blackfriars Bdge., Elephant & Castle, Kennington Pk. Rd. (ret. via Kennington Rd., WestminsterBdge) Clapham Com., Balham High Rd., Tooting High St., Merton Rd. — WIMBLEDON
4 (See also 2)	VICTORIA EMBKT.	Via:Kennington Rd. (ret. Kennington Pk. Rd., Elephant & Castle, Blackfriars Bdge.), Clapham Com., Balham High Rd., Tooting High St., Merton Rd. — WIMBLEDON
6 (Weekdays peak hours)	CITY (Southwark)	Via:Southwark Bdge., Borough High St., Kennington Pk. Rd., Clapham Rd., Clapham Com., Balham High Rd., Tooting High St., Mitcham Rd. — TOOTING (Amen Corner)
8 (See also 20)	VICTORIA STN.	Via : Vauxhall, Sth. Lambeth Rd., Clapham Com., Balham — TOOTING BDWY. Mitcham La., Streatham High Rd., Brixton, Stockwell, Sth. Lambeth Rd., Vauxhall — VICTORIA STN.
10	CITY (Southwark)	Via:Southwark Bdge., Borough High St., Kennington Pk. Rd., Brixton Rd., Streatham High Rd., Mitcham La., Southcroft Rd., Mitcham Rd. — TOOTING BDWY. Sat. aft. and eve.; Borough (St. Georges Ch.)-Tooting Bdwy only
12	LONDON BRIDGE	Via: Southwark St., Southwark Bdge. Rd., Borough Rd., Lambeth Rd., Albert Embankment, Nine Elms La., Battersea Pk. Rd., York Rd. — WANDSWORTH (High Street)
16 (See also 18)	VICTORIA EMBKT.	Via: Elephant & Castle, Kennington Pk. Rd. (ret. via Kennington Rd., Westminster Bdge.), Brixton Rd., Streatham High Rd., London Rd./ Croydon, Brighton Rd. — PURLEY
18 (See also 16)	VICTORIA EMBKT.	Via:Kennington Rd. (ret. via Kennington Pk. Rd., Elephant & Castle, Blackfriars Bdge.), Brixton Rd., Streatham High Rd., London Rd., Croydon, Brighton Rd. — PURLEY
20 (See also 8)	VICTORIA STN.	Via: Vauxhall, Sth. Lambeth Rd., Stockwell Rd., Brixton — TOOTING BDWY. Balham, Clapham Com., Sth. Lambeth Rd., Vauxhall — VICTORIA STN.
22 (Weekdays peak hours) (See also 24)	VICTORIA EMBKT.	Via:WestminsterBdge. Albert Embankment, Stockwell, Clapham, Balham High La. — TOOTING BDWY. Mitcham La., Streatham, Brixton, Stockwell, Sth. Lambeth Rd.,Westminster Bdge. — VICTORIA EMBKT.
24 (Weekdays peak hours) (See also 22)	VICTORIA EMBKT.	Via:WestminsterBdge. Albert Embankment, Stockwell, Brixton, Streatham, Mitcham La., Southcroft Rd. — TOOTING BDWY. Balham, Clapham, Stockwell, Albert Embankment, Westminster Bdge. — VICTORIA EMBKT.
26 26 26 26	LONDON BRIDGE	Via: Southwark St. BLACKFRIARS Victoria Embankment Westminster Bdge., Lambeth Palace Rd., Albert Embankment, Wandsworth Rd., Lavender Hill — CLAPHAM JUNC.
28	VICTORIA STN.	Via: Vauxhall Bdge. Rd., Vauxhall, Wandsworth Rd., Lavender Hill — CLAPHAM JUNC.
31	WESTMINSTER STN	Via:Westminster Bdge., Lambeth Pal. Rd., Albert Embankment, Wandsworth Rd., Nine Elms La., Battersea Pk. Rd. — BATTERSEA. Weekday peak hours: Extended Westminster Stn.-Bloomsbury, via Kingsway Subway
33	FINSBURY PARK (Manor House Stn.)	Via: Green Lanes, Essex Rd., Rosebery Ave., Theobalds Rd., Kingsway Subway, Westminster Bdge., Kennington Rd., Brixton Rd., Dulwich Rd., Herne Hill — WEST NORWOOD
34	BLACKFRIARS	Via: Blackfriars Rd., London Rd., Camberwell Rd., Coldharbour La., Stockwell Rd., Clapham Rd., Cedars Rd., Lavender Hill, Falcon Rd., Battersea Bdge. Rd. — CHELSEA (Kings Rd.)
35	HIGHGATE	Via: Holloway Rd., Upper St., Kingsway Sub., Rosebery Av., Victoria Embkt., Westminster Bdge., Kennington Rd., New Cross Rd., Malpas Rd., Brockley Rd., Stondon Pk., Park Rd. — FOREST HILL
36 (See also 38)	VICTORIA EMBKT.	(ret. via Blackfriars Bdge.) Old Kent Rd., Deptford Bdwy., Greenwich Rd., Woolwich Rd., Beresford Sq., Plumstead Rd., McLeod Rd. — ABBEY WOOD
38 (See also 36)	VICTORIA EMBKT.	Via: Blackfriars Rd. (ret. viaWestminster Bdge.), New Kent Rd., Old Kent Rd., Deptford Bdwy., Greenwich Rd., Woolwich Rd., Beresford Sq., Plumstead Rd., McLeod Rd. — ABBEY WOOD
40	VICTORIA EMBKT.	Via:WestminsterBdge., Kennington Rd., Camberwell New Rd., Peckham Rd., New Cross Rd., thence Route 36 — WOOLWICH (Beresford Sq.). Weekday peak hours: Extended Woolwich-Plumstead (Wickham Lane)
42	THORNTON HTH.	Via : Thornton Hth. High St., Brixton Rd.,London Rd.,North End, Croydon High St. — CROYDON (Greyhound)
44	WOOLWICH (Beresford Sq.) Weekdays	Via: New Rd.,Woolwich Common, Academy Rd., Well Hall Rd. — ELTHAM (High Street)
46	CITY (Southwark)	Via:WestminsterBdge., Marshalsea Rd., Gt. Dover St., Old Kent Rd., New Cross Rd., Lewisham Way, Loampit Vale, Lee High Rd., Eltham Rd., Eltham Hill, Well Hall Rd., Woolwich Com. — WOOLWICH (Beresford Sq.)

Right Remarkably, the northern entrance to the tunnel still survives, although bereft of its ornamental lamp standards and protected by a more substantial 'Keep Left' bollard! Looking down the 170-foot cutting in 1996 even the tram tracks and the central power conduit (overhead wires were not used) are still in place, and one of the lamp standards survives on the far parapet wall. It scarcely looks wide enough for two trams to pass! *WA*

This page **TEMPLE BAR**, between Fleet Street and the Strand, marks the western boundary of the City, and dates from the 13th century. Since the 16th century there has been a brief ceremony here when the sovereign obtains the Lord Mayor's permission to enter the City; he gives up his sword to the monarch, who returns it as a symbol that he or she is now under the Mayor's protection. From the late 17th century, when the Bar was a stone archway, the heads of executed traitors were displayed on it, and telescopes could be hired for a closer look; this was discontinued in 1746. In 1878 the arch was removed to ease the increasing traffic flow; it still survives, albeit in poor condition, at Theobalds Park, Cheshunt, Herts, and moves have recently been made to have it restored and returned to the City.

The present 30-foot-high monument was erected in 1880, and in the 1930s was still being considered 'a useless obstruction to traffic'; it is surmounted by the griffin, frequently but unofficially used as the City of London's emblem. The building on the left is what was originally Childs Bank, built in 1879; this company once had Nell Gwynne and Samuel Pepys amongst its customers. In the 'past' 1960s view a coach and an RT bus pass the memorial; in a little-changed scene, two modern buses do likewise in 1996. *Peter Townsend/WA*

Opposite page A few yards further along the Strand are the **ROYAL COURTS OF JUSTICE** (right), built between 1871 and 1882 to replace an area of notorious slums and to house all the superior civil (non-criminal) courts, although some criminal cases are also now heard here. There were 1,000 rooms, and the building, faced with Portland stone, used 35 million bricks. Extensions, the most recent in 1968, have brought the number of court-rooms to about 60. In 1996 its Gothic frontage is cleaned and once again sparkling white, accentuating the striking lines of the building.

Straight ahead is the tower of the church of St Clement Danes, an ancient foundation whose connection with the Danes cannot be explained with certainty. Although it survived the Great Fire, it was rebuilt by Wren in 1680-2. The interior was gutted during the war but restoration was completed by 1958 with financial contributions from Commonwealth and Allied Air Forces; it is now the central church of the RAF. Since 1957 the restored bells occasionally play the well-known nursery rhyme, so now again 'Oranges and lemons, say the bells of St Clement's (although the original St Clement's is possibly one nearer the river where Mediterranean fruits were once unloaded). Behind St Clements can be seen the roof of steel-framed Australia House, part of the Aldwych complex built in 1912-8.

Paris can be reached for £10 10s by Air France, and Nice for £25, according to the adverts on the RT bus in this June 1952 picture. The modern bus in the same position in 1996 is advertising the stage musical *Elvis* - 'the King' was still at school back in 1952! *London Transport Museum/WA*

This page At the other (west) end of the Aldwych, on the north side, is the **STRAND THEATRE**, which in 1980 was home to the world's longest-running comedy, *No Sex Please, We're British*. It had opened in June 1971 and by 1974 had become the theatre's most successful production; it closed after 6,671 performances in September 1987. In 1996 the theatre is showing another long-running hit, the musical *Buddy*, based on the life of singer Buddy Holly, which itself was then in its '7th heavenly year'.

The theatre opened as the Waldorf in 1905 with a season of Italian opera, becoming the Strand in 1912. The famous actor-manager Sir Donald Wolfit kept the theatre open during the war with lunchtime Shakespeare performances. Its post-war association with successful long-running comedies began with *Arsenic and Old Lace* in 1942, which ran for almost 1,400 performances (and which had been famously filmed in that year starring Cary Grant, Raymond Massey and Peter Lorre), and continued with *Sailor Beware* (1955, 1,082 performances), *A Funny Thing Happened on the Way to the Forum* (1963) and *Not Now Darling* (1968). *C. Mott, A. Mott collection/WA*

Opposite page At the extreme western end of Aldwych, on the corner of Wellington Street, is the **LYCEUM THEATRE**. This had originally been built in 1771, converted to a theatre in 1794, and Madame Tussauds first exhibited her waxworks here in 1802. The present building dates from 1831, and it was here that an unknown actor called Henry Irving first made his name in 1871. Irving mounted celebrated Shakespearean productions, and became manager in 1878, with Ellen Terry as his leading actress; he made his last appearance here as Shylock on 19 July 1902. Shortly afterwards all but the frontage was demolished and rebuilt as a music hall in 1904, but was immediately unsuccessful, and was taken over for the staging of melodramas. This lasted into the 1930s, but the theatre was then in severe decline. After the war, now under the ownership of the London County Council, it was let as a dance-hall, and in this guise it is seen in the late 1970s as Mecca's Lyceum Ballroom, presumably between shows. It finally closed in 1991.

In May 1996, the date of the second photograph, the Lyceum was being rebuilt as a theatre by Apollo Leisure, and it was duly re-opened on 31 October 1996 by the Prince of Wales. Paul Gregg, Apollo's Chairman, wrote in the commemorative brochure: 'The Lyceum Theatre has lain under the sword of Damocles for most of its three centuries of existence, after a number of fires, the closure for demolition as a site for a roundabout and the neglect over the last decade. . . Today, as you view the theatre, you call feel the history of Irving, Terry and Bram Stoker. You may remember the last decades as home to *Come Dancing* and *Miss World*, all very distant to the splendour of today's returned Lyceum Theatre.' The theatre re-opened with a revival of *Jesus Christ Superstar*. *C. Mott, A. Mott collection/WA (2)*

The rear cover of the brochure marking the re-opening of the Lyceum. *Apollo Leisure Group*

The area now known as **COVENT GARDEN** once belonged to the Abbey of St Peter at Westminster, then in the 16th century the land was granted to the 1st Earl of Bedford. The 4th Earl built Bedford House here, then to raise money he engaged architect Inigo Jones to design and build an elegant square of what became very sought-after houses, completed in 1639. In 1656 the market appeared as a few temporary stalls, then in 1670 the 5th Earl was given a Royal Charter for a fruit, vegetable, flower and herb market. By the mid-18th century it was large enough to attract com-

plaints, and by the beginning of the 19th century was becoming severely congested. Therefore in 1830 a new market place was built, with small lodges at the corners, one of which is seen here. The iron roofs were added in the 1880s.

In 1918 the whole site was sold by the then Duke of Bedford to a private company. Before the war about a million tons of fruit, vegetables and flowers were handled here annually by the 2,000 or so famous porters, who could carry upwards of 25 baskets balanced on their heads. In 1961 it was taken over by the Covent Garden Market Authority. Condemned in 1921 by the Ministry of Food as 'altogether inadequate', for 200 years alternative sites had been suggested, but finally in 1966 a new site was identified south of the river at Nine Elms, and in 1974 the market closed.

Between 1975 and 1980 the buildings were restored by the GLC, and reopened as shops and restaurants and the popular venue for a host of street entertainment activities. The 'past' view, taken on Wednesday 27 May 1970, shows a bustling scene of porters with barrows and hundreds of boxes, crates and sacks of produce. On Good Friday 1996 a fairground is the attraction at the far end, in front of the Flower Market of 1870-1, which since 1980 has housed the superb London Transport Museum, whose Photo Library is the source of many excellent photographs reproduced in this book. *Neil Davenport/WA*

At the northern corner of Covent Garden stands the **ROYAL OPERA HOUSE**. The original theatre was built in 1732, and saw the piano played for the first time in public (1767) and the premières of Goldsmith's *She Stoops to Conquer* and Sheridan's *The Rivals*. Following its destruction by fire, a new building replaced it in 1809. The first performances in English of Mozart operas were given in the early 19th century, and after a decline in fortunes in the 1820s, it reopened in the 1840s as the Royal Italian Opera, and Verdi's works received their premières. The present building dates from 1858; in the 1880s electric lighting was installed, and at the turn of the century Puccini's operas were being premièred. After the First World War operas were sung increasingly in English, but again the building's fortunes waned and in 1929 its leased expired, and it was threatened with demolition. However, it survived with Sir Thomas Beecham as Artistic Director. During the Second World War it was used as a dance-hall, then in 1946 it became the National Opera House. Its resident companies were granted Royal Charters in 1956 and 1968 to become the Royal Ballet and the Royal Opera respectively.

Just after this circa 1980 photograph was taken a multi-million-pound expansion was started beyond the theatre towards Floral Street (unseen here), opening in 1982 and providing new rehearsal studios and dressing-rooms. Otherwise little has changed except for the completion of the building in the background in Long Acre; the motor cycle stand is still prominent. The wider 1996 view is intended to show the Floral Hall next door with its Eliza Doolittle/*My Fair Lady* associations. Built in 1860, it was damaged by fire in 1956, and the arched glass roof and dome had to be removed. Both Hall and Opera House were designed by the same architect, but what a juxtaposition!

Since the 'present' photograph was taken the area on the left has become a huge building site for a major redevelopment that will also face on to Covent Garden Market. *C. Mott, A. Mott collection/WA*

This page These two pairs of pictures on this spread demonstrate the kind of social, as well as to some degree architectural, changes that have been wrought in London in the last few decades. In November 1967 **TOWER COURT**, off Tower Street near Seven Dials, is apparently a nondescript row of rather dilapidated early-19th-century houses, with a 'copy shop' on the far corner. Blotting out the sky in the background is Thorn House (1957-9) in Upper St Martin's Lane. The area around Seven Dials had long been a very disreputable area, and even as recently as the early 1970s Pevsner could describe it as the 'closely packed district of vice and crime into which it [has] deteriorated'.

However, all that was to change with the Covent Garden scheme, following the closure of the market. A draft plan was published in 1970, with council housing, schools and community buildings, and the preservation of a 'character route' through the area. This became the very popular and attractive maze of small streets around Neal Street and Neals Yard, now full of arts and craft shops, specialist restaurants and all the trappings of fashionable 1990s Covent Garden. Tower Court itself, as can be seen, has been 'gentrified', for want of a better word - the houses have been refurbished and repainted, shrubs and flowers planted in containers, and 'traditional' street lighting added. So dense is the greenery that a slightly different angle had to be used. The

premises behind the iron railing are no longer a drab yard, but now belong to the Really Useful Company, with which Prince Edward is associated. *Neil Davenport/WA*

Opposite page The second view is of **GREAT QUEEN STREET**, the continuation of Long Acre towards Kingsway. It was laid out at about the same time as Covent Garden in the 1630s, and was described as 'the first regular street in London'. The original buildings have gone, unfortunately, but some early-18th-century ones survive (including those on the right of the picture), while Nos 36 and 37 are late 18th century. However, in November 1967 it could almost be a row of shops in the suburbs of any city. On the left is Malangone's grocery and confectionery shop, very much an 'Open All Hours' establishment! Next door is a rather forbidding-looking 'medical eye centre', then a 'Sandwich Coffee Bar' that has not quite brought itself into the Swinging Sixties. At No 34 R. A. Miles is a jeweller.

In 1996 an entirely different ambience pervades the area. Malangone's shop is a smart Indian Restaurant, the eye centre a fashionable hat shop, the sandwich bar another Indian restaurant, No 34 a hair-stylist, and next door is Danny's Bar, a coffee bar very much a part of the '90s. All in all it is a very telling contrast. *Neil Davenport/WA*

Opposite page 'It is the highway of the world,' claimed Arthur Mee before the war. 'In some mysterious way this commonplace thoroughfare draws every traveller to it.' The 1940 Red Guide adds: 'The intelligent traveller has only to pause in any doorway to watch the crowds of all ranks, ages and conditions and nationalities that surge by, to have an epitome not merely of metropolitan but of national and world life.' This is the **STRAND**, parallel to but higher than the Embankment. By the 12th century, if not earlier, it was a path alongside the river, hence its name. Later its south side was to contain the houses of noblemen, with gardens going down to the water's edge; following the building of the Embankment it is, of course, now some way from the water. In the 1890s there were more theatres here than anywhere in London, and by the early years of the present century it was renowned as a place of public houses, restaurants, music-halls and fashionable recreation.

The 'past' view, taken on Monday 16 May 1966, shows a convoy of Routemaster buses heading eastwards, with predominantly taxis moving towards Trafalgar Square; Nelson's Column can be seen on the horizon. Unfortunately we were not able to gain access to the upper storeys to achieve the exact equivalent angle, but in 1996 a Routemaster (which was already a couple of years old when the 'past' picture was taken!) is still plying the 13 route, with another on the 6 behind it.

The building in the centre dates from 1903-4, following the widening of the Strand, and is Savoy Buildings; the entrance to the famous Savoy Hotel, behind it and nearer the river, is tucked away in Savoy Court, with the round turrets on the corners. The building's distinctive facing is a creamy, matt-glazed terracotta by Doulton. On the ground floor is the famous Simpson's-in-the-Strand restaurant, dating from the 1840s and famous for sumptuous roasts wheeled in on dinner wagons. It is still a highly regarded restaurant and distinguished meeting venue serving fine traditional foods.

Beyond the Savoy is the former Cecil Hotel, now the Strand frontage of Shell-Mex House (see page 37); it was the largest hotel in London when it opened in 1886. In 1996 'Character shoes' is up for letting, and the former Woolworths is now partly a Boots store. *London Transport Museum/WA*

This page We are now at the western end of the **STRAND** looking back towards the Cecil Hotel (the building with the twin towers on the right) in 1954. Prominent on the right is the Halifax Building Society of 1933, then at the end of the following row the Tivoli cinema, built on the site of a music-hall that had opened in 1890 and closed in 1914; the cinema opened in 1923. Subsequently the site was built on again in 1957-9, when the building seen in the 1996 view was erected; originally Peter Robinson's store, it is now the New South Wales Government headquarters; in 1954 they occupied the premises next door to the Halifax. In the far distance is the church of St Mary-le-Strand, below Aldwych. The buildings on the extreme right were soon to be demolished (as seen on the opposite page), and the road made to a uniform width to remove the strange 'kink'.

Note parked outside the Halifax a Daimler ambulance of the early 1950s, immortalised in the early die-cast Dinky toy! Apparently only a handful are known to exist today. Passing the number 9 RT bus on the pedestrian crossing is a large American car, followed by an AC, a taxi and another RT on route 6; in the foreground, travelling in the other direction, is an elegant 'half-convertible' *sedanca de ville*. Today the pedestrian crossing (still host to numbers 9 and 6 buses!) is controlled by lights, and unauthorised crossing nearby positively discouraged, such is the enforced segregation of cars and people in today's capital! *London Transport Museum/WA*

Opposite page 'Strand widening scheme - these premises to be demolished - First and Last Sale' declares one of the condemned buildings on the corner of Villiers Street and the **STRAND**. It is 1956 and what is possibly the last block of 'old' Strand buildings is to be pulled down to complete the widening beyond the Halifax building (tucked behind the end of the block on the right). Amongst other firms selling up are a restaurant, the Strand photographic studios, and pawnbrokers Vaughan's at No 39 on the corner of Buckingham Street. Demolition of the near end appears already to have started, but the exposed end of the buildings (war damage?) has been oddly painted to represent medieval castle walls complete with trees!

On the subject of the above-mentioned street names, a house on this site once belonged to George Villiers, Duke of Buckingham, hence the existence in the locality of George Court (now York Buildings), Villiers Street, Duke Street and Buckingham Street - there was even an Of Alley at one time (now York Place)!

A brand new development on the corner, Villiers House, opened in late 1996. Note how the Halifax building is now exposed, on the same line as the new development. On the extreme right can be seen one of the gate-posts of Charing Cross station. With virtually no traffic and no road markings, the Strand of 1956 looks positively peaceful compared with the 1996 snarl-up! London sees a traffic flow of an average of over 28,000 vehicles a day, and the average speed of traffic in the capital is little more than 10 mph, whether during the rush hour or off-peak. *N. L. Browne, courtesy of Frank Hornby/WA*

This page Located at the end of the Strand and close to Trafalgar Square, **CHARING CROSS** is considered one of those nodal places where the full pageant of London life will pass before anyone who lingers there; as Dr Johnson (who else!) said, 'I think the full tide of existence is at Charing Cross.'

Stepping to the south-west end of the station forecourt we can see the monument that gives the district its name. In the 13th century Charing was a tiny village west of London, and when in 1290 King Edward I's wife Eleanor died in Nottinghamshire, he had 12 crosses erected at the places where the funeral procession rested on its way south to Westminster Abbey; this was the last. Unfortunately the original was demolished after the Civil War in 1647. At the Restoration of the monarchy in 1660 eight of those who has ordered the execution of Charles I were themselves beheaded here. When Charing Cross station was built on the site in the 1860s, the South Eastern Railway paid for a replica of the Cross to be erected in the forecourt, where it stands today, now beautifully cleaned.

In the June 1956 photograph the exposed end of the Villiers Street corner site can again be seen, and on the left, on the other side of the Strand, is the frontage of the 'West Strand Improvements' of 1830-2 planned by Regency architect John Nash. Redeveloped internally in the 1970s, most of the frontage and the 'pepper-pots' at each corner of the triangular site were retained. The part completely remodelled was the centre portion, Coutts's Bank, just behind the Cross. As can be seen from the 'past' view, the building inserted in 1903 was completely out of character, and has now been replaced by a dramatic glass-screened frontage of the same height as the rest of the building. This May 1996 view was taken before the wraps came off Villiers House. *A. J. Pike, courtesy of Frank Hornby/WA*

The **PLAYERS THEATRE** in Villiers Street had it origins in the Players' Theatre Club founded in 1927, which had various homes in the West End until it moved into two arches beneath Charing Cross station (seen here circa 1980), which had formerly housed a music-hall. Back in 1936 Leonard Sachs, co-founder of the Players, had conceived the idea of recreating Victorian music-hall, and it was members of the company that formed the chorus when Sachs and the very popular *The Good Old Days* moved on to television via the stage of the City Varieties Theatre, Leeds. However, it was a production of *The Boy Friend* that opened the new theatre in 1953.

The recent building of the new office premises astride the station (see pages 26-7) meant the Players Theatre moving to temporary premises between 1987 and 1990. Today the frontage is totally transformed by the new Coopers & Lybrand building, No 1 Embankment Place, but echoes of the railway arches are seen in the design of the entrance. *C. Mott, A. Mott collection/WA*

Today access to the Players Theatre is from the passage that runs beneath the station from Villiers Street to Craven Street, and music-hall is once again the order of the day. *WA*

Past and Present colour
Central London

SELFRIDGE'S, OXFORD STREET: 'Selfridge's is one of the finest architectural spectacles in London. . .,' sings Arthur Mee in the 1951 London volume of *The King's England*. 'We meet wonder at the very door, for above it is London's most wonderful clock.' Seen clearly in this photograph, the 'ship's prow' is surmounted by the 'Queen of Time' bearing on her shoulders the huge clock, the whole being some 24 feet high. In all, 7 tons of bronze are supported on the 15-ton block of stone; the hour bell alone, struck by two winged figures, weighs 3 tons.

Ever since it opened its doors on Monday 15 March 1909, Selfridge's department store has attracted extravagant statistics - the building, with its massive Ionic columns, is 170 yards long and 60 deep, with 30 lifts and escalators even in the 1950s, when the store used more electricity in a year than Dover! American retailer Gordon Selfridge was backed by Sam Waring of Waring & Gillow, on the understanding that Selfridge would not compete with him by selling furniture. At 1.05 pm on a sunny Saturday 27 July 1963, a Green Line 'Routemaster' and London Transport 'RT' bus pass the store, with a motor scooter, Ford Anglia and Mini adding further period detail. The familiar green buses disappeared at the beginning of 1970 when they were nationalised as London Country, a National Bus Company subsidiary.

In April 1996 it is pleasant to report that wider pavements have squeezed what remains of the traffic - buses and taxis only - into a much narrower thoroughfare, allowing easier strolling between Oxford Street's famous shops. The mass of Selfridge's still dominates, with even more greenery cascading from the upper storeys, while many new trees also now soften the scene. From the early 1970s there were plans to make the street a 'tree-lined paradise'; the new pavements, bus shelters and plantings around Selfridge's were completed at the end of 1993. *Frank Hornby/WA*

This shopping guide to London, dating from just after the war, includes Selfridge's, 'The Heart of London Shopping': 'Those who know Selfridge's intimately, recognise it as an Institution, dedicated to the service of the shopping public, and founded upon the highest principles of goodwill and integrity.' *Authors' collection*

The elegance of John Nash's original **PICCADILLY CIRCUS** was destroyed as early as 1886 when Shaftesbury Avenue, seen here piercing the north-east side, was built, turning the Circus into an awkwardly irregular junction - a 'horrible shape' as Eros's disgruntled sculptor Sir Alfred Gilbert called it. (The statue was erected to the memory of the philanthropist 7th Earl of Shaftesbury - note how the bow is angled downwards to *bury* the *shaft*.)

By the turn of the century shopkeepers were discovering the attraction of illuminated advertisements, which were soon erected in profusion, the London County Council unable to prevent them; the famous Bovril and Schweppes signs appeared in 1910. This sunny view from July 1964 contains a wealth of detail: the 'First British Circlorama Film' on the left, then beneath the famous Coca Cola ad one for British European Airways' Trident jet, introduced in 1962. The Guinness Clocks, this one complete with the familiar seals and toucans, were once an essential part of the Piccadilly scene, while a brand new VC10 is just emerging from its scaffolding above, having first flown in April 1964.

There's hardly a British name to be seen in lights in Piccadilly Circus in March 1996, replaced by Japanese and American electronics and fast food, and Australian lager! Such is the effect of the 'global village' of the 1990s. . . The greatest transformation, though, is the reshaping of the Circus from a traffic roundabout - the erstwhile 'Hub of the Empire' - to a one-way semi-circle around the top. As can be seen, in the 1980s Eros was moved bodily some yards to the east and is now accessible without having to negotiate the traffic. The London Pavilion on the extreme right has been shorn of its adverts and cleaned, and in the distance is the bulk of the unlovely and unloved Centre Point, built between 1963 and 1967.
Frank Hornby/WA

Like Piccadilly Circus, **TRAFALGAR SQUARE** is one of the great London landmarks and meeting-places, especially for political rallies and New Year's Eve celebrations! This 1959 view of the north side shows the wall that was necessary to 'terrace' the square (the site being on a slope) in order to pave the area and erect Nelson's Column in 1839-42. Set beneath the wall are brass measures giving the exact imperial measures of inch, foot, yard and chain. Beyond, the Square is dominated by the National Gallery.

Surprisingly the two well-known fountains were added almost as an afterthought a few years later. Originally fed from wells beneath the National Gallery, they are now electrically powered from the mains. The fountains were remodelled in 1939, and only after the war were the mermaids and dolphins added.

Loss and gain characterises the 1996 view. The trees atop the north terrace have gone, but behind the fountain, on an area of land empty since 1949, is the new Sainsbury Wing of the National Gallery. Three Sainsbury brothers, of supermarket fame, offered to finance the building in 1985. Designed by Venturi, Rauch & Scott Brown and completed in 1991, it attracted the famous 'carbuncle' quote from the Prince of Wales, but looks well enough in this view. Even the original 1838 building provoked criticism - it was said that the central dome and end pavilions looked like the clock and vases on a mantlepiece!

Note that the bus is advertising the stage show of Pete Townshend's rock opera *Tommy*, the hit album first released in 1969, still 10 years in the future when the 'past' picture was taken! And during 1959 rock'n'roll singer Marty Wilde had four big hits in a row, including 'Donna' and 'Teenager in Love'; his daughter Kim, born the following year, is starring in *Tommy*. . . *Frank Hornby/WA*

Linking Trafalgar Square and Westminster is **WHITEHALL**, named after a Tudor Palace and now synonymous with the seat of British Government. It's hard to believe from the width of the road today - at 130 feet, the widest in London - that in former times it was a notorious bottleneck for carriages; Pepys records in 1660 that a footman was killed in a 'falling out' between coachmen - so 'road rage' is nothing new!

The large building on the right is occupied by the Ministry of Defence and was newly completed when the 'past' photograph was taken on a sunny Saturday 3 October 1959. A large and unusual

building, architectural historian Nikolaus Pevsner considered that the four towers looked like 'two-storeyed houses . . . stranded high up'. At the right of the picture is the Red Lion pub, a Victorian replacement for an earlier establishment, while in the middle of the road is the famous Cenotaph ('empty tomb') commemorating 'The Glorious Dead', where Armistice Day services have been held since it was erected in 1920. Recognising that the servicemen and women it remembers were of all creeds and none, architect Sir Edwin Lutyens omitted all religious imagery.

Today the 77A bus still plies Whitehall and little has changed, except perhaps for the cleanliness of the stonework of some of the buildings in a now smokeless capital. There's more traffic, of course - and double yellow lines - and today's cars are rather more plush than yesteryear's Ford Zephyr and Popular! *Frank Hornby/WA*

Whitehall becomes Parliament Street more or less where the previous photographs were taken, then enters the north side of **PARLIAMENT SQUARE**, laid out in 1868 as a suitable approach to Parliament, and remodelled in the 1940s. This superb 1959 view was taken from the top deck of a bus entering the Square from Abingdon Street, and we are looking up Whitehall.

The building on the corner of Parliament Street and Bridge Street (leading to Westminster Bridge) is interesting, in that the 'present' picture looks more 'past' than the 'past' one! When built it had a cupola turret on the corner, but by 1959 this had been lost and replaced by a dreary modern tiled roof with out-of-character dormer windows. In 1991, however, the whole building was refurbished to provide parliamentary accommodation, and much more attractive upper storeys and cupola re-instated. Note another significant difference between the two rooflines - in 1996 a forest of surveillance cameras scans Parliament, which, coupled with the very obvious parking ban, sadly reflects the concerns of the security-conscious 1990s. The ground floor is now the Houses of Parliament gift and book shop.

The buildings next door in Bridge Street have been demolished, facilitating the underground construction of the Jubilee Line extension. The new building for the site will be the result of an architectural competition held in the early 1970s. The building on the left is the Edwardian 'New Government Offices', while on the extreme right can be glimpsed a corner of Westminster Hall.

The differences in traffic and its management in the intervening decades are obvious, but note in 1959 the splendid Standard Vanguard 'Beetleback' following the Bedford lorry into Abingdon Street, and the Bond three-wheeler turning into the Square. *Frank Hornby/WA*

Moving now to the other end of the central London area covered by this book, we find ourselves on London Bridge looking at **NEW FRESH WHARF** on the north bank. Until about 1800 every ship coming up the river had to unload all dutiable cargo at this stretch of docks; this caused great congestion and delay, and pilferage was rife. When larger docks were built down-river of the Tower in the early 19th century, the Upper Pool, as this part of the river is known, declined in importance. By the early years of this century the previous Fresh Wharf was the starting point for the Belle and General Steam Navigation pleasure steamers, which made daily trips to Southend, Margate and Ramsgate, and even as far afield as Lowestoft and Boulogne.

On Wednesday 13 May 1959 MV *Alfonso* is berthed at the quay, which is apparently laden with sacks of produce. On the extreme left is a corner of Adelaide House of 1924-5, while just to the right of the Wharf warehouse can be seen the columned turret of the Coal Exchange in Lower Thames Street, and behind it the tower of Sir Christopher Wren's St Dunstan-in-the-East, the only part of the church to survive wartime bombing. The building on the right is part of Billingsgate Fish Market.

A dramatic transformation greets the visitor on 5 April 1996! The warehouses and cranes have gone, and the wharf now carries a pair of striking modern office buildings, St Magnus House (1980, centre, taking its name from another of Wren's City churches, now revealed behind it) and Montague House (blue glass, 1986). Even the bridge beneath the photographer's feet is different, having been rebuilt in 1967-72. Billingsgate Market was closed in 1982 and moved down-river to the Isle of Dogs, the Coal Exchange was demolished in the 1960s, but St Dunstan's survives, now glimpsed against the dramatic roofline of Minster Court (1986-90). *R. C. Riley/WA*

Swinging the camera round to the right, we are now looking at the south bank of the river, which was still quite busy with wharves and shipping when this photograph of the tug *Tudorose* and its raft of empty lighters was taken on Friday 21 June 1957. **HAY'S WHARF**, stretching from Tower Bridge to London Bridge, was begun in 1651 by Alexander Hay, and is the Port of London's oldest. Cold storage was pioneered here, with New Zealand dairy produce being handled as early as the 1860s. The named building on the right dates from 1931-2, in the very 'modern' style of the day with bronze-framed windows and 'jazz' period sculptured panels. Note how it is raised on columns to allow easy access to the wharf.

The Hay's Wharf building is listed, so has survived the otherwise dramatic redevelopment along the shore, symbolising London's new commercial environment - from cranes to computers, shipping to service industries. Chamberlain's Wharf, built in the 1860s, has become the London Bridge Hospital, and further down river is the very fashionable Hay's Galleria - obscured by cranes in the industrial landscape of 1957 - its arched, glazed roof housing shops and eateries. Although the river still handles a modicum of commercial shipping, this March 1996 view has a modern 'City Cruise' vessel in place of the tug, and the only 'cargo' now handled at Hay's Wharf is riverboat passengers at the new pier. *R. C. Riley/WA*

Another famous London landmark to have made the transition from commerce to leisure is **COVENT GARDEN MARKET**, seen here on a Wednesday morning in May 1970, during its last few years as London's best-known fruit and vegetable market. Built on the site of the produce garden of the Convent of St Peter at Westminster, the market dates from 1656, when it was held in part of the garden of the Duke of Bedford's house. Later he remodelled the area into an Italian-style 'Piazza', which was rather spoiled by the addition of the market in the centre in 1670. The present buildings were erected in 1830, when the market also became popular as a place for the fashionable to mingle with the country folk and flower-sellers. The green building in the background is what remains of the Floral Hall of 1858, damaged by fire in 1956 - the familiar tale of *Pygmalion/My Fair Lady*'s Eliza Doolittle immediately comes to mind - and beyond it the mass of the Royal Opera House.

The site belonged to the Duke of Bedford until 1918, when it was sold to a private company. Sold again in 1961, the market survived until 1974, when its inadequacies finally led to a move to a larger site at Nine Elms, south of the river. The Greater London Council restored the buildings and they reopened in 1980 to become one of London's most fashionable shopping, eating and street entertainment venues. On Good Friday 1996 the lorries, barrows and crates of fruit and veg have been replaced by a busy and colourful travelling fairground. *Neil Davenport/WA*

Before moving into Trafalgar Square, we return briefly to the river, and the **VICTORIA EMBANKMENT** near Waterloo Bridge. A riverside road was first proposed by Sir Christopher Wren after the Great Fire, but it was not until 1864-70 that it was built on 37 acres reclaimed from the Thames and enclosed behind a high wall. Beneath the road run the tracks of the District and Circle underground lines. This June 1952 picture was taken a few months after the closure of the Kingsway tram tunnel, which entered the Embankment under the arch of Waterloo Bridge on the extreme left. The replacement buses on the 171 and 172 routes were diverted via Aldwych and the Temple at street level to gain the Embankment.

Trams ran along the Embankment from Blackfriars Bridge to Westminster Bridge, crossing both to gain the southern suburbs, the southern and northern networks having been linked via the tunnel from 1908. A tram can be seen heading towards the bridge on what was one of the few reserved stretches of track in London, segregated from other traffic. Before the war 400 trams an hour served the Embankment, with 500 passengers a minute leaving by tram during the rush hours.

Neither trams nor buses run along the Embankment today, and the full width of the road is utilised as a spacious dual carriageway, allowing tourist coaches to park under the trees beside the river. However, the street lights are still strung across the road on span wires, as they were over 40 years before. *London Transport Museum/WA*

Opposite page This is the view of the north side of **TRAFALGAR SQUARE** from the steps of St Martin-in-the-Fields. Again, it is one of London's great focal points, conceived by John Nash, with a road entering from the east (Pall Mall East, at the far end of the Square in this picture) and one from the west (Duncannon Street towards the West Strand Improvements at Charing Cross). But nothing came of his plans for the north side, until Charing Cross Road arrived awkwardly in the north-east corner in the 1880s. Where the National Gallery now stands was the King's Stables, and St Martin's Place (foreground) was the narrow lower end of St Martin's Lane, which ran right down to the Strand. However, all these ramshackle buildings were demolished to make way for the new Square in 1830. The sloping site was exploited by having the north side as a terrace, with steps down into the Square. Above was built the National Gallery, founded in 1824 and built here in 1832-8; from its origin in 38 masterpieces purchased for £57,000, it now houses well over 2,000 pictures.

In this splendid 'past' view dated Thursday 10 September 1953, what might be a Wolseley passes in the foreground while a vintage half-cab coach turns into St Martin's Place. A survey before the war found that this was the second busiest spot in London, with 66,000 vehicles passing through in 12 hours. Today traffic and pedestrian management is more sophisticated, and the roads well marked with lanes. On the skyline, to the left, Canada House has acquired a new roof extension (visible now that the older trees have been replaced by new saplings), and in the centre rises New Zealand House. The distant buildings in Pall Mall East are now obscured by the new Sainsbury Gallery, added in 1985-91 (see also page 117 and the colour photographs).

In the far corner of the Square (hidden by trees and traffic), is a plinth that has stood empty since the Square was laid out, because no one could decide who or what to put on it. In July 1996 a solution was

announced: the Royal Society proposed that a different statue should occupy the site each year for five years - one Victorian, one early 20th century and three to be commissioned. Back in the 1930s Arthur Mee wrote: 'The empty pedestal is waiting for a hero: surely it is the very place for the Chief Scout on his horse.' In the 1990s suggestions have included Lady Thatcher, Nelson Mandela and footballer Paul Gascoigne. We suppose it depends on one's idea of a hero. Watch this space... *C. F. B. Penley, A. Mott collection/WA*

This page We are now looking at the north side of **TRAFALGAR SQUARE** from the other end, in Pall Mall East, the 'past' picture having been taken on Tuesday 22 June 1954. On the left is, of course, the National Gallery, the statue this time being James II, and the background is dominated by St Martin-in-the-Fields. This famous church has its origins in the 13th century, when it would have been very much 'in the fields'! The present building was

erected in 1722-6, with its distinctive 'temple front' portico surmounted by a steeple, a design new in England and much copied in America. Buckingham Palace is in its parish, and it has seen many Royal christenings in the past. The crypt was used as a shelter for homeless people after the First World War, and as an air raid shelter during the Second; damaged by bombing, it has since been restored and is used for concerts and meetings, as well as housing the London Brass Rubbing Centre.

On the extreme right in both pictures is the northern portico of Canada House, while the removal of the trees reveals in 1996 the distant cranes atop the Villiers House development in the Strand. Note how the former uncontrolled pedestrian crossing with its central refuge has been replaced by a controlled crossing without a refuge; even though the pavement on the right has been widened considerably, it's an awful long way across when the 'bleeps' are sounding! *C. F. B. Penley, A. Mott collection/WA*

This page Feeding the pigeons in **TRAFALGAR SQUARE** is a traditional London pastime, but it isn't enjoyed by everyone, and there is a certain amount of conflict between the custodians of the Square. The Planning & Environment Committee of Westminster City Council feel that the pigeons should be discouraged - by a ban on feeding and the use of 'birth control' pellets as used elsewhere in Europe - as they are a health risk to children and a cleaning problem for the borough. However, the Square is under the control of the Department of National Heritage, which considers that it should be an exception because of the tradition. Certainly there seem to be fewer pigeons in 1996 than are seen in the 'past' picture taken on 16 January 1965. But birdseed is being sold in vast quantities from both kiosks, in tins in 1965 but now in paper cups. And while the situation was turning Major General Sir Henry Havelock prematurely white in 1965, that seems less of a problem today!

In the left background (hidden by trees in 1996) can be seen the tower of the Coliseum, built in 1904 as a variety theatre; the globe on top used to revolve. It is now London's largest theatre, the first in England to have a revolving stage and the first in Europe to have lifts. In the 1960s it became a cinema, but in 1968 reopened as the new home of the Sadler's Wells Opera Company, which was renamed the English National Opera. On the right is South Africa House of 1935. *Arthur Davenport/WA*

Opposite page 'Here we are at the heart of things,' wrote Arthur Mee of **TRAFALGAR SQUARE** in the 1930s, 'between Piccadilly and the Strand, with Whitehall down to Westminster in front, the National Gallery behind, Canada facing South Africa across the Square. . .' This is the view from the North Terrace, the past picture taken on Wednesday 29 August 1951. In the foreground is one of the two famous fountains, not part of the original design and only completed in 1845; they were remodelled in 1939, when the mermaids and mermen were added. The southeast corner of the Square seen here used to be occupied by the large square Jacobean London mansion of the Dukes of Northumberland, but this was demolished in 1874 and replaced by Northumberland Avenue and the present buildings. In the 1970s Pevsner described them as 'two big shabby Late Victorian buildings . . . fussy, commercial, without much dignity or character', but they have been considerably improved in recent years by cleaning and refurbishment, especially that on the left, originally the Grand Hotel. The site was to have been redeveloped, but refurbishment was chosen after a campaign in the *Architects' Journal*. Removal of the advertising hoardings has also helped.

The view down Whitehall (right) towards the Houses of Parliament is impressive, and on the extreme right can be seen two of the four great lions guarding the foot of Nelson's Column; they are 20 feet long and 11 feet high and arrived very late in 1867 (their non-appearance a standing joke in the newspapers of the day), while the column itself, raised in 1839-42, is 170 feet high, surmounted by the 17-foot-high figure of Nelson. *Arthur Davenport/WA*

Opposite page The winding **ST MARTIN'S LANE** was laid out in the 17th century, leaving the Strand at what is now the bottom of Trafalgar Square and at this point becoming Monmouth Street and leading up to Seven Dials. It was once the site of large and fashionable houses occupied by the likes of furniture-maker Thomas Chippendale, painter Sir Joshua Reynolds and actress Ellen Terry. All of that was part of history by 1953, when the 'past' picture was taken. At the bottom of the road can be seen the steeple of St Martin-in-the-Fields and the globe-topped tower of the Coliseum. At the junction of St Martin's Lane with Long Acre, Cranbourn Street and Garrick Street the road widens. On the left is a rather blank-looking building housing the Sussex pub, since extended and now accommodating Stringfellows famous restaurant, but hidden by the trees in the 1996 view (which unfortunately had to be taken from street level since the building from which the earlier one was taken is closed and due for redevelopment). On the left, part of the former St Martin's Hotel was pulled down to make way for Wellington House and a garage car park in 1960, while on the right the assorted early buildings were replaced by the slab of Thorn House in 1959, recently refaced.

The 'present' view, while not from the same angle, gives a good idea of today's one-way traffic congestion, whereas in 1953 taxis could be parked in the middle of the road, and a horse-drawn dray could plod along unmolested. Are today's pavements wider, or the cars just much bigger? The 1950s picture is full of interest and detail, including what appears to be a recent visit from a water-cart, spraying as near to the edge of the road as the parked vehicles permit. *C. F. B. Penley, A. Mott collection/WA*

This page **CHARING CROSS ROAD** runs roughly parallel to St Martin's Lane, and this is a scene at the bottom end behind the National Gallery. Centre stage in this 6 August 1972 picture is an RT bus on the 176 route. The RTs were in their last few years of service - they ended their days deep in the east London suburbs at Barking, where the last one ran in April 1979.

In the left distance can be seen the Talk

of the Town, opened in 1900 as the London Hippodrome, a combined music-hall and circus with a built-in water tank. In 1996 it is obscured by modern buildings, but in both views can be seen the horse sculpture on the roof ('hippodrome' being a Greek term for a racecourse for horses and chariots). For many years a successful variety and revue theatre, it became the Talk of the Town 'Theatre Restaurant' from 1958 to 1991. It is currently the Hippodrome Disco, offering dancing from 9 pm to 3.30 am.

In 1996, as a modern de-regulated Grey-Green bus passes the same spot, the Peabody Trust, in association with The Housing Corporation, is renovating the block on the right to provide 22 flats as affordable rented accommodation, a children's nursery and two shops. The Trust was set up in 1862 with a £500,000 donation from American philanthropist George Peabody to 'ameliorate the condition of the poor and needy of this great metropolis. . .'. By 1890 the Trust had over 5,000 dwellings in inner London, often rather austere buildings but a great boon in their day; today it still owns and manages nearly 12,000 properties on 72 estates. Note that the Gold Coin Exchange, beside the bus in 1972, is still in business amongst the building works in 1996. *R. C. Riley/WA*

Halfway up Charing Cross Road is the intersection with Shaftesbury Avenue at Cambridge Circus, location of the **PALACE THEATRE**. Built in 1888-90, with much terracotta embellishment, as The Royal English Opera House under Richard D'Oyly Carte, it was demoted to the Palace Theatre of Varieties the following year, adopting its present name in 1911. Becoming particularly associated with musicals, *Song of Norway* was staged here in 1946, and Ivor Novello's *King's Rhapsody* in 1949. *The Glorious Days* was the show in Coronation year, 1953, and was an apt patriotic musical vehicle for Anna Neagle, although it was a critical flop. It was in effect a collection of old song hits (such as 'Soldiers of the Queen' and 'K-K-K-Katie') strung together to 'allow Miss Neagle to move gracefully through her island story . . . in a series of tableaux, some not terribly vivant,' as Sheridan Morley described it. Miss Neagle played several historical roles, including Nell Gwynne and Queen Victoria (she became particularly associated with the latter role, playing Victoria on screen three times). Better-received musicals at the Palace have included Laurence Olivier in *The Entertainer* in 1957, Norman Wisdom in *Where's Charley?* (the musical version of *Charley's Aunt*) in 1958, and *The Sound of Music*, which ran for 2,385 performances from 1961 to 1967. From 1972 to 1980 Rice and Lloyd Webber's *Jesus Christ Superstar* became the longest-running musical (3,357 performances) until their own *Cats* broke the record. *Les Miserables*, 'The World's Most Popular Musical', opened in 1985, and was in its 11th record-breaking year in 1996. *C. Mott, A. Mott collection/WA*

104

Both **CHARING CROSS ROAD** and Shaftesbury Avenue were laid out in the 1870s/1880s as badly needed improvements in communications between Piccadilly Circus/Trafalgar Square and Bloomsbury. Some of the buildings, most very undistinguished architecturally, were erected to house 900 people displaced by the new Northumberland Avenue. In these views, looking north from Cambridge Circus, there are two particular buildings of interest, one small and one large.

In the very bottom right-hand corner of the 'past' photograph, taken on Saturday 13 February 1965, can be seen the shop of Marks & Co at No 84, which was immortalised in Helene Hanff's book *84 Charing Cross Road* (Andre Deutsch, 1971). It tells 'the very simple story of the love affair between Miss Helene Hanff of New York and Messrs Marks & Co, sellers of rare and second-hand books.' The book consists simply of the lively transatlantic correspondence between Miss Hanff and Frank Doel of Marks's between 1949 and 1969 and the growing friendship between the two that grew up over the years. For anyone who has read this little classic (or seen the stage adaptation or the 1986 film starring Anne Bancroft and Anthony Hopkins), the fact that Frank Doel is probably inside that shop in February 1965 is very moving. He died in December 1969 without the two of them ever having met. Helene came to London in 1971 to help promote the book and visited the now empty shop. It's a very poignant story and recommended to anyone with a passion for old books, for which Charing Cross Road is of course famous. Helene Hanff herself died in April 1997 aged 80.

The other building is the 35-storey, 398-foot-high Centre Point in New Oxford Street, built between 1963 and 1967. Something of a massive architectural white elephant, the fact that it remained empty for over a decade caused great controversy. Edward Jones and Christopher Woodward, in their *Guide to London Architecture,*

write: 'Land speculation has been central to the development of London since the 17th century. . . However, when private speculation is not constrained by consensus on desirable forms of development it contains the seeds of destruction for the city. Centre Point is London's most conspicuous monument to this fatality.'

Note that the traffic is moving one way up the road; this was part of the largest one-way traffic experiment ever tried in Central London, introduced on Sunday 30 April 1961 and involving a network of 3 miles of streets from Cambridge Circus to the top of Hampstead Road/Gower Street. 'The Minister of Transport, Mr Ernest Marples, hopes you will co-operate in making the experiment a success,' requests a contemporary leaflet. *Frank Hornby/WA*

'Charing Cross Road is a narrow, honky-tonk street, choked with traffic, lined with second-hand bookshops. . . We got out at 84. Deutsch's had stuffed the empty windows with copies of the book. Beyond the window the shop interior looked black and empty. . . The two large rooms had been stripped bare. Even the heavy oak shelves had been ripped off the walls and were lying on the floor, dusty and abandoned. I went upstairs to another floor of empty, haunted rooms. The window letters which had spelled Marks & Co had been ripped off the window. . .

I started back downstairs, my mind on the man, now dead, with whom I'd corresponded for so many years. Halfway down I put my hand on the oak railing and said to him silently: "How about this, Frankie? I finally made it."'

The Duchess of Bloomsbury Street, Helene Hanff
(Andre Deutsch, 1974)

6. WESTMINSTER

Opposite page There's barely a brick or a chimney-pot to distinguish these two views, taken almost 40 years apart, of one of London's most venerable sites, **HORSE GUARDS PARADE**. The 1940 Red Guide describes it as 'the largest "clear" space in London (if a space can be described as "clear" which is largely used for the parking of cars). . .'. Our 1959 view shows no cars parked, and entry to the area for the few authorised vehicles in 1996 is strictly guarded. In 1959 it appears that stands are being erected, or perhaps dismantled, for the Trooping of the Colour, which has taken place annually here in June, on the monarch's official birthday, since 1805; the monarch also takes the salute. (The purpose of 'trooping the colour' is the parading of regimental colours in front of the troops so that they will recognise them on the field of battle.) The colours are those of the various Guards of the Household Division, and the Queen took the salute on horseback until 1986.

The area was used in Tudor times for tilting, and from the 17th century for parades of various kinds. The Horse Guards building itself was built in 1750-60, with what Pevsner refers to as its 'restless recessions and projections', surmounted by a clock tower; it is the headquarters of the Household Division of Guards and the London District Army Command. The buildings, from left to right, are Admiralty House (brick, 1780s), the former Paymaster General's Office, Horse Guards, Dover House, and the Cabinet Offices. Lord Wolseley and Lord Roberts survey the scene from their horses. *Frank Hornby/WA*

This page In its entry on **HORSE GUARDS**, the Red Guide continues: 'A passage under the picturesque clock tower . . . is much frequented by foot-passengers, but only royalty and a few privileged persons on the Lord Chamberlain's list are allowed to drive through.' Certainly while we were attempting to take the 'present' picture we were interrupted by official cars entering through the gates from Whitehall, which were opened by the Life Guard who was thoughtfully posed to take the place of the two 'squaddies' in the 12 September 1953 picture! In the lodges on either side of the gate, facing out into Whitehall, are mounted Horse Guards providing a famous and very patient tourist attraction!

Again the various buildings do not appear to have altered in the slightest degree in more than four decades. The building on the left with the circular columned corner is the old War Office of 1907, that on the right part of the Banqueting House begun by Inigo Jones in 1619; in the centre background is Whitehall Court, built as flats in 1884. *C. F. B. Penley, A. Mott collection/WA*

At the bottom of Whitehall is Parliament Street, leading into **PARLIAMENT SQUARE**, where this superb photograph was taken on Saturday 20 April 1957, looking north up Whitehall. Imposing government offices stand on the left, while on the right, on the corner of Bridge Street, is a building that has undergone an interesting transformation. As described in the colour photographs, the building originally had a squat dome on the corner (*left*, circa 1902) and gabled windows in the roof, but at some time prior to 1957 the upper storeys were removed and the very inappropriate tiled roof substituted. Then in 1991 the building was refurbished and upper storeys more in keeping with the original were replaced - the result is that the 1996 building looks more 'past' than the 'past' one! Where Noel's menswear shop was on the ground floor is now the Houses of Parliament book and souvenir shop. The buildings next door in Bridge Street have been demolished to facilitate the construction of the Jubilee Line extension, and for the same reason the Parliament Square island itself has been 'boxed in'.

The first 'traffic lights' in Britain were installed here in 1868; invented by a railway engineer, they stood 23 feet high, had semaphore arms attached and were controlled manually. In 1957 there's no sign of any, and a couple of policemen on point duty appear to be doing the job! In 1996 the traffic control is very complex, extending also to controlled pedestrian crossings. Security is also sophisticated, with a forest of surveillance cameras on the roof on the right, and a ban on unattended cycles. A traffic warden (introduced to London in 1958) also helps to keep everything moving! Note the BEA '1½-decker' airport bus in the 1957 photograph. *Frank Hornby/WA*

Is this the most famous view in London? Certainly the chimes of **BIG BEN**, via the radio, have symbolised home, civilisation, The Empire or whatever for many generations of Britons! Although popularly known by that name, 'Big Ben' is in fact the nickname only of the great hour bell, perhaps named after the Chief Commissioner of Works during the rebuilding, Sir Benjamin Hall. The clock mechanism is over 15 feet long and 4 ft 7 ins wide and weighs about 5 tons. The faces are 22 ft 6 ins in diameter and are made of translucent glass lit from white walls 5 feet behind them; the minute spaces are 1 foot square. The original cast iron hands were found to be too heavy for the mechanism to move, so were replaced by gunmetal ones. The minute hand still fell alarmingly when it passed the 12, so a lighter hollow copper one was used instead; it travels over 100 miles a year! The hour bell was cast at Whitechapel and weighs 13½ tons; the new hour begins on the last stroke.

The clock was started on 31 May 1859, and it used to take two men 32 hours to wind it every eight days until automatic winding was introduced in 1913. The 13-foot pendulum is regulated by adding or removing old pennies. Even the bombing of Parliament in 1941 only caused a 1½-second discrepancy! Three of the clock faces were reglazed in 1956, and in 1968 the 320-feet-high tower was found to be out of vertical by 9½ inches, but no further movement has been detected.

The 'past' view was taken at 4 pm on Sunday 26 April 1959, so there's not a lot of traffic and, again, minimal traffic control. By

contrast, at 4 pm on Wednesday 29 May 1996 there's rather more! The 'Keep Left - one way only' sign reminds us that such arrangements are a relatively modern phenomenon, as described in the Introduction.

The pictures show again the new corner dome on the building on the left, and the old St Thomas's Hospital buildings across Westminster Bridge that have been replaced. *Frank Hornby/WA*

This is the east side of **PARLIAMENT SQUARE** looking south on Monday 12 July 1954. On the left is the vehicular entrance to the Houses of Parliament, and the roof of Westminster Hall, the only part of the original building to survive the disastrous fire on the night of 16 October 1834. The Hall was incorporated when the new Gothic Palace of Westminster was built; the foundation stone was laid in 1839 and the final part, the mighty Victoria Tower (seen here, 336 feet high), was completed in 1860. The part in scaffolding is the gatehouse-like St Stephen's Porch, the usual public entrance.

On the right is the east end of first St Margaret's church, today gleamingly cleaned, then the magnificent Henry VII's Chapel of Westminster Abbey, also now returned to its original glory (its elaborate architectural decoration inspired Pugin and Barry, the new Palace's designers). Note that since 1954 Millbank Tower of 1963 (see page 32) has appeared on the skyline. Traffic lights, road markings and the greater informality of the pedestrians' dress in 1996 are otherwise the main differences between the two views. *C. F. B. Penley, A. Mott collection/WA*

Above A London Underground poster explaining the developments at Westminster, on the site just off the right-hand side of these pictures. *WA*

The north-east corner of the Houses of Parliament facing Westminster Bridge and the **VICTORIA EMBANKMENT** is the Speaker's residence, and it forms a distinguished backdrop to this photograph taken on 4 July 1952 during London's 'Last Tram Week'. All that week Londoners had been crowding on to the trams in an atmosphere of carnival mixed with sadness. Just before midnight on 5 July the last tram made its final journey from Woolwich to New Cross, cheered all along its route despite the hour. It arrived at New Cross half an hour late, and was driven into the Depot by the Deputy Chairman of London Transport, packed inside and completely surrounded by heaving crowds. However, while London's tram tracks now fell silent, 92 'Feltham' trams had been sold to Leeds at £735 apiece in 1950, and they continued in service until that city's tramway was in turn abandoned in 1959.

John R. Day, in *London's Trams and Trolleybuses*, sums up: 'The tram was in many ways even more the "people's transport" than the bus, partly because its cheap fares brought it into the reach of almost everyone. It was utilitarian for much of the time, its rails threw you off your bicycle, it occupied the centre of the street and refused to get out of the way, and yet we loved it. Its 6d fare to anywhere, after 18.00, could transform it into a magic carpet for the impecunious youngster wanting to explore his London. There was no thrill like that of a roaring, squealing, brightly lit tram rushing down a cobbled, gas-lit street on a slightly foggy winter evening. London is not the same without its trams and the older ones among us recall them with deep feelings. . .'

Note that the tram has a trolley pole on its roof, but that it is fastened out of use while current is being obtained via a collector that ran in a slot in the conduit in the road. When the tram reached a point where overhead wires supplied the current, the pole would be raised.

It is appropriate that the 'present' view of the same spot (where London's third horse tram route began in 1861) should show a further development in London's transport, the Jubilee Line extension from Westminster to Docklands. The upper part of the Jubilee Line was built as the Fleet Line between Baker Street and Charing Cross via Bond Street, using part of the Bakerloo Line; it was renamed in 1977, and opened in 1979. In 1989 approval was given for the extension from Green Park to Stratford, east London. *London Transport Museum/WA*

In more relaxed times public car parking was permitted outside the Houses of Parliament in **OLD PALACE YARD**, but today security considerations mean that it is strictly controlled. On 22 September 1956 we can see a fairly new Mark 1 Ford Zephyr Zodiac and on the left a much older black Austin 10/4; today's cars are obscured by the metal railing.

Rising above them is the mounted statue of Richard I, the Lion Heart, and behind him Barry's magnificent window in the south wall of St Stephen's Porch, opposite the entrance to St Stephen's Hall and its great dais at the south end. The porch and lamps on the right mark the Peers' Entrance. Old Palace Yard takes its name from the original palace of Edward the Confessor, and it was here on 31 January 1606 that Guy Fawkes and his fellow Gunpowder Plot conspirators were executed. *Frank Hornby/WA*

This is the south side of **PARLIAMENT SQUARE**, looking towards Broad Sanctuary on the left, and beyond it Victoria Street; the date is 12 July 1954. Note first of all how the simple bollards at the junction with Old Palace Yard were all that protected cars and pedestrians; today the 'red and green men' and stout railings protect the unwary. Again, in 1996 the No Waiting sign and warning about leaving unattended pedal cycles remind us of modern security considerations.

In both pictures light vans are heading towards the Middlesex Guildhall of 1906-13. This was once the site of the Sanctuary Tower where fugitives from justice could find refuge, but this was abolished in 1623. Ancient Middlesex - the county of the Middle Saxons - lost much of its area to the County of London in 1888, and disappeared altogether in local government terms in March 1965, when it was absorbed into the administrative area of Greater London. However, quarter sessions are still held in the Guildhall. Glimpsed

through the trees on the left is the Methodist Central Hall (see page 116), and on the extreme left the tower of St Margaret's church. In 1996 the Parliament Square island is fenced off for the Jubilee Line extension works. *C. F. B. Penley, A. Mott collection/WA*

THE ONLY
FULL LENGTH FILM OF
THE CORONATION IN
GLORIOUS TECHNICOLOR
including
the Crowning Ceremony
in Westminster Abbey

A QUEEN IS
CROWNED

Colour by TECHNICOLOR

ODEON LEICESTER SQUARE
ON THE NEW WIDE SCREEN
from JUNE 6th
and in
ALL LONDON RELEASE AREAS
week commencing JUNE 8th

In 1953 **WESTMINSTER ABBEY** is ready for the Coronation of Queen Elizabeth II on 2 June. The building against the West Front is the Coronation annex, designed by Ministry of Works architects; the entrance was at the left-hand side under the circular canopy beneath which hung a huge Royal coat of arms. It was here that the young Queen arrived in the magnificent State Coach to a roar of cheers and a fanfare of trumpets, despite the dreadfully wet weather, and from here that she departed to return to Buckingham Palace, wearing the Imperial State Crown and carrying the Orb and Sceptre; as her carriage left the Abbey the head of the procession, snaking through London, was already in Hyde Park, 2 miles away.

Back in May 1936 the Coronation of King George VI has been seen on television by a limited audience (from Cambridge in the north to Brighton in the south). The *BBC Handbook* of 1938 says: 'Mobile television was gloriously inaugurated on Coronation Day. Despite bad weather conditions, the whole of the Coronation Procession was televised from Apsley Gate, Hyde Park Corner, and it is estimated that more than 10,000 people found the opportunity to see the picture on a television screen. . .'

In 1953 many more were able to watch the event on TV, although there were only about 50,000 sets in Britain; 40 years later 98 per cent of British households possesses a television, of which 95 per cent are colour. Despite the technical limitations of the era, the biggest television audience to date sat enthralled by the chalky flickering pictures of the ceremony. There were establishment figures who were against the televising of the service, but those in favour prevailed.

The day ended with a night of celebrations, reaching their climax in a gigantic firework display on the South Bank, a highlight of which was a set piece portraying the Queen, the Duke of Edinburgh and their two children. For those without television, and who were used to seeing their news at the cinema, a full length Technicolor film was on release within days, narrated by Sir Laurence Olivier.

Although the Abbey dates from at least the 11th century - William the Conqueror was crowned here on Christmas Day 1066 - the great West Towers were not completed until 1745. The column in the foreground is a memorial to members of Westminster School who died in the 'Russian and Indian Wars' of 1854-9, including Lord Raglan of Charge of the Light Brigade fame. Passing the column in 1953 is a splendid Triumph Roadster (familiar more recently from the TV series *Bergerac*), and parked next to it an L Series Vauxhall.

After the Coronation, in 1954-6, a gift shop was established in front of the Abbey, but the most striking contrast between the two pictures is the cleaned stonework, which completely transforms the building - what a pity the atmosphere was not clean enough for it to be done in 1953! *N. L. Browne, courtesy of Frank Hornby/WA*

Looking across the open space beside Westminster Abbey, through which Broad Sanctuary passes diagonally, we can see the Methodist **CENTRAL HALL** in Storey's Gate. This was built in 1905-11 in the ornate French style, an early example of the use of reinforced concrete. This gives the view a distinctly continental look compared with the pomp and solidness of other Victorian/Edwardian institutional buildings in the area. It is noteworthy as the first meeting place for the infant United Nations in 1946.

Fifty years later the buildings flanking it have all been replaced; that on the left, formerly Abbey House of 1859 with its pavilion roofs, is now NIOC House, housing Barclay's Bank on the ground floor behind its elaborate detached concrete tracery, while on the right is The Queen Elizabeth II Conference Centre. Three of the five trees have survived the more than four decades since the 'past' picture was taken on 12 July 1954. *C. F. B. Penley, A. Mott collection/WA*

7. ROYAL LONDON

PALL MALL formed the western exit from Trafalgar Square in Nash's 'great improvement' of the area from Carlton House to Regent's Park. It is seen here from the steps outside the National Gallery, the 'past' picture dating from Thursday 10 September 1953. On the left is Canada House, now cleaned and with a further storey added to its roof. Across the road the twin-towered building is Kinnaird House of 1915-22, and rising behind it the very inappropriate 225-foot, 15-storey tower of New Zealand House at the bottom of Haymarket, built in 1957-63.

In the right foreground the most dramatic addition to the scene, replacing what appears to be a post-war complex of single-storey shops, is the new Sainsbury Wing of the National Gallery. In 1985 brothers Sir John, Simon and Timothy Sainsbury offered to finance an extension to provide a home for the Gallery's collection of Early Renaissance works, as well as an auditorium, conference rooms, shop and restaurant. The various designs submitted provoked the Prince of Wales's famous 'carbuncle' remark, but that accepted, by architects Venturi, Rauch & Scott of Philadelphia, USA, was completed in 1991. Standing in front is a statue of King James II. Note that the elegant gas-lamp standards of 1953 have been removed, but that a lamp has been replaced on the post beside the steps in the foreground. *C. F. B. Penley, A. Mott collection/WA*

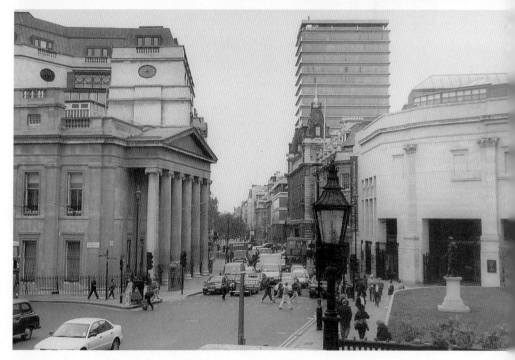

Opposite page We are now standing in the centre refuge of the pedestrian crossing in **PALL MALL** looking back towards Trafalgar Square, and at once the atmosphere of London's 'Clubland' is apparent - in the architecture and the cars! In June 1956, although virtually all the visible vehicles are Ford or BMC (Austin/Morris) products, it is the splendid Rolls-Royce on the left that catches the eye! In the 1996 view Fords and taxis still predominate, but we waited in vain for a Rolls. . . The cyclist on the right - of which there are still many in London - is wearing a mask to filter the fumes.

In the distance can be seen the dome of the National Gallery, and Canada House to the right. In 1956, on the left, was the 'New Zealand Migration Offices', including the former premises of cigarette company 'Rothman's of Pall Mall' (with blind). Founded in Fleet Street in 1890 by Louis Rothman, whose family owned a tobacco factory in the Ukraine, the firm moved to Pall Mall in 1900 and is now further down at No 65. That whole block was replaced by New Zealand House. Next door to Rothman's is the arched entrance to Royal Opera Arcade (which still survives in 1996). This was London's first shopping arcade, and was designed in the Parisian fashion by John Nash and built in 1816-8.

On the extreme right, the first building is the former United Service Club, built by Nash in 1827 immediately after the demolition of Carlton House and remodelled in 1842; in 1996, freshly repainted, it houses the Institute of Directors. Behind the camera Pall Mall proper starts at Waterloo Place, and beyond are the famous clubs such as the Athenaeum, Reform, Brooks's, Boodle's, etc. Note how the road markings in this one-way street have developed in 40 years. *London Transport Museum/WA*

This page From the 16th to the 19th centuries **ST JAMES'S PALACE** was one of London's principal Royal residences (the only one when Whitehall Palace burned down in 1698). Originally built by Henry VIII in the 1530s on the site of a remote leper hospital, the only surviving part is the gatehouse (the clock and turret on the skyline) facing Pall Mall. The present-day buildings behind, seen here, are brick, built following a fire in 1809. Queen Victoria was the first monarch to move into the newly refurbished Buckingham Palace (see pages 124-5), but foreign ambassadors are still accredited to 'the

Court of St James', although they are actually received at the Buckingham Palace.

Perhaps not surprisingly, nothing has changed in four decades in this view looking up Marlborough Gate towards Pall Mall, except perhaps a few TV aerials; the lamp on the right is the same, and even the inspection cover in the pavement in front of it! The RT bus in the 1950s 'past' picture is on diversion, as no regular buses use Marlborough Gate. In 1996 it is replaced by two mounted police officers, while a party of American tourists, having 'debussed' in Pall Mall, make their way down to The Mall to see the Changing of the Guard. In the background can be seen the premises of Hardy's, makers of fishing tackle, established in 1872 in Alnwick, Northumberland, and located in Pall Mall since 1892. *A. J. Pike, courtesy of Frank Hornby/WA*

Pall Mall takes its name from a game of Italian origin, *palla a maglio* ('ball to mallet'), or *palle-maille* in French, which involved hitting a ball with a wooden mallet through a suspended iron hoop some distance away. 'A paille mall is a wooden hammer set to the end of a long staff to strike a boule with, at which game noblemen and gentlemen in France doe play much,' was a 1621 description. Pall-mall was once played by Charles II and his mistresses in the vicinity, then part of the park of St James's Palace, then in 1660 the alley was moved to a new half-mile-long, fenced-in, tree-lined site, and that eventually became **THE MALL**. Indeed, 'mall' eventually became a general term for any shady, tree-lined walk, and in our own time, via the USA, an undercover shopping precinct - the 'maul' of American TV!

In time The Mall became a popular promenading area for fashionable society folk, even after the game that gave it its name was no longer played. Surprisingly, however, the road that we know so well today only came into being in 1903-11. It was laid out as a 65-foot-wide route to the south of the original 'Mall' (now the parallel horse ride) joining Buckingham Palace with the new Admiralty Arch, built in 1910 (see overleaf), and at last solving the capital's embarrassing lack of a really impressive processional route.

Since 1911 many Royal occasions have including a procession along The Mall, and these are reflected in the accompanying pictures. In the first (*top*) we see the 65-foot triumphal arches erected in May 1953 for the following month's Coronation. It was along here that the 2-mile-long procession, with its 10,000 marching men and women, came as the new Queen returned to Buckingham Palace on 2 June. Note the Irish-registered Ford Prefect in the bottom left-hand corner - perhaps over here for the celebrations?

On Friday 29 April 1960 (*middle*) the banners are out to mark the Royal Wedding on 6 May of Princess Margaret and Anthony Armstrong-Jones (who became Lord Snowdon the following year).

Today's view (*bottom*) shows, of course, little change except perhaps in the growth of the trees, and road markings have appeared at the traffic lights at the junction with Marlborough Gate. *N. L. Browne, courtesy of Frank Hornby/C. F. B. Penley, A. Mott collection/WA*

Above right Thousands upon thousands of Londoners and visitors were crammed along the route of the Coronation procession, and their transport by trolleybus, road and rail was a major undertaking, commencing at 3 am!

HOW TO GET THERE
LONDON TRANSPORT
CORONATION DAY
SERVICES

BUSES TROLLEYBUSES and GREEN LINE COACHES

London Transport's central area buses to the Coronation Terminals inside the Coronation Area and trolleybuses going near to the Coronation Area will start from about 3 a.m. in order to arrive from 4.30 a.m. onwards. Green Line coaches will be timed to begin arriving at the Coronation Terminals between 5 a.m. and 6 a.m.

All services to the Coronation Terminals will display labels in the colours of the sections of the Processional Route they serve.

There will be special early morning and late night bus and trolleybus connections in the outer areas to link with the train services at many suburban stations, and all-night bus and trolleybus services will be increased to about four vehicles an hour.

There will be early morning journeys on certain country area bus routes to link with outer main line suburban stations and with Green Line coach routes.

Last buses home will leave the Coronation Terminals at about 1.30 a.m., last Green Line coaches at about 12 midnight, and last trolleybuses from the central area at about 1.30 a.m.

CONSULT THE CORONATION MAP
and see notices on the vehicles concerned

LONDON TRANSPORT RAILWAYS

Trains will start running from most outer terminal stations at 3 a.m., stopping at most stations until full services start at 5 a.m.

The following stations will be **closed all day** :—Aldwych, Arsenal, Caledonian Road, Cannon Street, Drayton Park, Great Portland Street, Kensington (Olympia), Mornington Crescent, North Ealing, Regent's Park and Shoreditch ; also Covent Garden (until 6.30 p.m.) and West Brompton (until 5 p.m.).

The following stations will be **restricted** until after the Procession :— Charing Cross, Green Park, Holborn (Kingsway), Marble Arch, Piccadilly Circus and Strand — see special posters at stations for details.

The following stations will **not open until after the procession** :— Bond Street, Hyde Park Corner, Trafalgar Square and Westminster.

Special late trains home from the central area will run until about 1.30 a.m. throughout Coronation week, except to stations beyond Rickmansworth and from Moorgate to Finsbury Park.

CONSULT THE CORONATION MAP
and special posters at London Transport stations

The Coronation Folder Map is obtainable free at Station Ticket Offices, Enquiry Offices and Police Stations, or you can write to or call at the office of the Public Relations Officer, London Transport Executive, 55 Broadway, Westminster, S.W.1.

Above In June 1977 the Queen's Silver Jubilee was another occasion for which The Mall was decorated. As for the Coronation, rain was a feature of the day, but as always it failed to dampen the spirit of the huge crowds. These two views, looking towards Admiralty Arch (*top*) and Buckingham Palace, give some idea of the effectiveness of The Mall as a ceremonial route.

The Royal Wedding processions of Prince Charles and Lady Diana Spencer in July 1981, and Prince Andrew and Lady Sarah Ferguson in July 1986, also passed this way, but with the subsequent very public separations and divorces, the apparently changing attitude of the people to the monarchy, and its own perception of its future role in the light of recent self-reforming initiatives, will there be fewer such joyful occasions along The Mall in years to come? *Both WA*

Left Playing at pall-mall in the 17th century. *Authors' collection*

ADMIRALTY ARCH was erected in 1910 as the magnificent formal gateway at the eastern end of The Mall. The Latin inscription is King Edward VII's tribute to his mother, the Arch forming part of the national memorial to Queen Victoria. In this delightful 'past' photograph, again taken in Coronation Year, 1953, the Arch is suitably decorated, and on the right, on both sides of the Arch, can be seen some of the stands erected to accommodate 100,000 people, and containing 700 miles of tubular steel. The fashions of the day are well illustrated by the couple on the right, while heading towards the Arch on the left are, amongst others, a Citroen and an open-top Sunbeam. Today the cleaned Arch and refurbished buildings beyond produce a much brighter scene, although with no Coronation imminent in 1996! The central gates are only opened on ceremonial occasions. *N. L. Browne, courtesy of Frank Hornby/WA*

At the other end of **THE MALL** is the Queen Victorian Memorial in the centre of Rond Point, the 'circus' in front of Buckingham Palace. This was a product of the same Queen Victoria Memorial Committee that had instigated the Mall improvements. The area was to represent the 'hub of the Empire', and was designed by the same man who was responsible for Admiralty Arch and the new Portland stone frontage of the Palace. All was ready for the Coronation of King George V in 1911. The statue of Queen Victoria, facing down The Mall, is 13 feet high, made from a single block of marble and surrounded by allegorical figures such as Justice, Charity, Truth, Victory and Manufacture; the whole

ensemble swallowed up well over 2,000 tons of stone. In the 'past' photograph, again dating from the Coronation of 1953, the statue is boarded round to protect it, and one of the triumphal arches can be seen as a mother and daughter venture gingerly into the road.

Car parking is certainly not encouraged in 1996, and the junction at Buckingham Palace is protected by traffic lights. Here, though, is at least one London thoroughfare where cars have no choice but to give way to horses, as a company of Guards process eastwards following the Changing of the Guard. Note again how much cleaner the Palace is today. *Des Saunders/WA*

Despite being seen as the focal point of the British monarchy, **BUCKINGHAM PALACE** as a Royal residence is of relatively recent origin. Buckingham House was built in 1702-5 for the 1st Duke of Buckingham. In 1762 George III bought it for £28,000, but it was his son, George IV, who saw it as the new Royal residence, Carlton House being insufficiently grand; he engaged John Nash to repair and improve it. The work began in 1826, but when Queen Victoria came to the throne in 1837 it was still not really habitable. It was finally completed, with the construction of the 360-foot east front (to The Mall, giving Victoria and Albert more accommodation) in 1847; the enclosure of that front necessitated the removal of the former gateway - the Marble Arch - to its present site at the top of Park Lane (see page 139).

The Palace only received its familiar present-day frontage in 1913. Forty years later, in Coronation year, it can be seen that the Portland stone has suffered badly at the hands of the London atmosphere, but in 1996 it can once again present a clean face to the inevitable crowds who always seem to be there waiting for something to happen, or a glimpse of the Royal Family. In the 1993 view (*left*) they will be unlucky, the absence of the Royal Standard on the flagpole indicating that the Queen is not in residence. The Guards protecting the Palace can be watched, of course, and most mornings the Changing of the Guard provides a fine tourist spectacle. Note in the 1953 and 1993 views the happy matching juxtaposition of the taxi and cars (in 1953 a Morris and an Austin Somerset, in 1993 a brace of Audis).

Even the 1993 view is now 'past', because in 1995 a 'pedestrian plaza' was created outside the gates; like Piccadilly Circus (see pages 146-7), Rond Point is no longer an island, with traffic travelling in both directions round one side only. 'How splendid,' said a spokeswoman for the Pedestrians' Association. 'Now that pedestrians are given priority and recognition in one of the seats of power, they will feel enthused to achieve the same in the towns where they live.' Some 17 million people go to the Palace each year, and in the previous three years 60 sightseers had been hurt in traffic accidents outside. The traffic lobby was less impressed, of course, but the development was awarded a Civic Trust commendation in March 1996.

Since 1993, to help pay for restoration following the disastrous fire at Windsor Castle, certain of the 600-odd rooms in the Palace have been open to the public for the first time. *Des Saunders/WA (2)*

Buckingham House as it was in 1775 before the remodelling of the 1820s and '30s and the addition of the east front to complete the quadrangle in 1847. *Authors' collection*

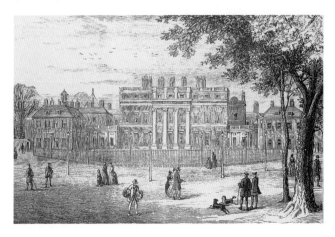

8. VICTORIA PANORAMA

We start by looking north towards our last port of call, Buckingham Palace. In the 'past' view, dated (as all these are) Thursday 29 September 1960, the whole of the Palace can be seen (middle distance just to the left of the head of the crane); the older west front faces the garden, while at the right-hand end is the familiar east front, which completed the quadrangle in 1847.

In front of the Palace can be seen the Queen Victoria Memorial surrounded by the gardens and ornamental gateways of Rond Point. The whole is backed by the trees of Green Park, bordered on the north side by Piccadilly.

The whole area on the north side of this end of Victoria Street was redeveloped between 1960 and 1966. The 6-acre site used to be occu-

WESTMINSTER CATHEDRAL in Victoria Street is the centre of the Roman Catholic Church in Britain, and while Victoria is only on the fringes of the area covered by this book, the view from the Cathedral's 273-foot-high campanile tower does afford spectacular views of many of the areas we have already visited, so the following panoramas are included for that reason.

The building was only completed as recently as 1903, designed in the Early Christian Byzantine style. Because finances were limited, the interior decoration was left for future generations to complete, a process still going on today. Development in Victoria Street led to demolition of property in front of the Cathedral in 1971, leaving an open area that allowed its distinctive frontage to be viewed fully for the first time. Because of its relatively recent date, the campanile contains a passenger lift, so taking the 'present' pictures was not so arduous a task for your authors as the laborious ascent of the spiral staircases of St Paul's and the Monument! *WA*

pied by Watney's Brewery, built about 1860 and demolished a century later in 1959. Bounding the site to the north-east is Palace Street with its Georgian cottages and assorted other buildings; the south side of the street was all demolished for the Stag Place development, which hides most of the view today. The building in the foreground is Esso House, which was eventually to swallow the remaining Victorian apartment block. Beyond the Esso flagpole on the extreme left can be seen the Hilton Hotel in Park Lane. On the right horizon is the British Telecom (formerly Post Office) Tower, opened in 1965. It has a total height of over 600 feet, and is 1¾ miles away from Westminster Cathedral (as we are told by the helpful plaques in each viewing gallery). *C. F. B. Penley, A. Mott collection/WA*

When Victoria Street was cut through the area of slums between Westminster Abbey and Victoria station between the 1850s and 1880s, it was remarkable for the evenness and uniformity of the height of its buildings. These were described as 'mansions', many divided into 'flats', a wholly new innovation in London at that time. Others contained blocks of 'chambers', many forming the offices of the prominent Victorian civil and mechanical engineering companies that built and supplied the railways. The five-to-seven-storey blocks are seen clearly flanking the street in the 1960 view, looking now north-eastwards; note the hundreds of chimney-pots that once contributed to the characteristic London 'pea-souper' fogs!

In the 1996 view the uniformity has been taken to extremes! Kingsgate House presents a blank face to Victoria Street, while tucked behind it in the bottom left-hand corner is the Gothic brick of Westminster City School. At the right of the picture is the 19-storey slab of Westminster City Hall.

Bisecting the middle distance is the band of trees marking St James's Park. Just in front of them at the left-hand end is the long low rake of Wellington Barracks on Birdcage Walk, reconstructed in 1979-82. At the right-hand end in 1960 is the 14 storeys of 'that irredeemable horror' (Pevsner) known as Queen Anne Mansions, 'rudely bare . . . grimy brick walls and uniform windows'. It was built and part-designed by a property developer between 1873 and 1889, and mercifully demolished in 1971-2. The tallest building on the modern horizon is Centre Point. *C. F. B. Penley, A. Mott collection/WA*

Earlier we spoke of the horizontal layers of London, each age laying down new strata over the remains of the previous ones. These three views seem to demonstrate *vertical* layers, where successively taller buildings obscure the view of earlier ones behind. On 29 September 1960 (*above*) there is a clear view eastwards towards Westminster, characterised by the almost uniform scale of the major buildings. The large white block in the left middle distance is Broadway House, built in the late 1920s as the headquarters of London Transport. At 175 feet high, the clock tower made it at that time one of London's tallest and most 'modern' buildings! A little further to the right can be seen the large dome of Central Hall (see page 116), and above and slightly to the left the dome of St Paul's Cathedral, 1½ miles away. Right again the Shell Tower on the South Bank is under construction, then the tip of the tower of Big Ben can be seen directly behind the West Front of Westminster Abbey. The Houses of Parliament stretch as far as the Victoria Tower on the right. Directly beneath the Shell Tower, in Victoria Street, is the prominent 'crowning monstrosity' (Pevsner) of Windsor House (1880s), 'a nightmare of megalomaniac decoration', while the tiny building next door to it, on the corner of Buckingham Gate, is The Albert pub. In the centre foreground is the famous Army & Navy Store, linked by three footbridges to further premises in Howick Place.

By the date of the second photograph (*above right*, a close-up of the centre of the view taken on 23 July 1967), Victoria Street westwards has been entirely rebuilt, the Westminster City Hall block on the extreme left, then the ten storeys of Mobil House. In the centre middle distance is the 20-storey tower of the 'new' New Scotland Yard completed in 1966. On the skyline the Shell Tower was completed in 1963, and in front of Westminster Abbey in Victoria Street is the Department of Trade and Industry building, completed in 1964 and replacing Westminster Chambers of the 1860s.

The earlier views have by 1996 (*right*) been almost entirely blotted out by a forest of new buildings. On the left Westminster City Hall is partly hidden and the rest of Victoria Street obscured behind the distinctive 'glass building-block' design of Ashdown House (undergoing refurbishment), while two new blocks now completely hide New Scotland Yard and the Shell Tower; both in Buckingham Gate, the dark one of the left is No 65, the Registered Office of Rolls-Royce Ltd, and the other is the modern-day Windsor House. Right again is Southside, the new 1977 building housing the Army & Navy, with just one footbridge across Howick Place.

Despite its present gleaming whiteness, Westminster Abbey is almost lost to view, while to the left of Victoria Tower can be seen the new block of St Thomas's Hospital across the river. On the far horizon is the City, a sierra of office blocks, of which St Paul's is the merest molehill! *C. F. B. Penley, A. Mott collection (2)/WA*

We are now looking roughly south-westwards towards the train sheds of Victoria railway station. In the foreground, running left to right, is Carlisle Place, then immediately behind it and parallel, Vauxhall Bridge Road. The light-coloured building in the left middle distance is the rear of the Apollo Victoria, formerly the New Victoria Cinema of 1929. Threatened with demolition in 1971, it was reprieved and now stages musicals and comedies. In 1996 Lloyd Webber's *Starlight Express* was the hit; the word 'Andrew' can be seen on the building in the 'present' picture.

Behind again are the roofs of Victoria station, which was in fact built as two stations side by side, one opened by the London, Brighton & South Coast Railway in 1860, the other by the London, Chatham & Dover Railway two years later. At the right-hand end of the station are the station offices, and behind them the French-style Grosvenor Hotel of 1861, one of London's first railway hotels, being cleaned in 1996. (Incidentally, Grosvenor is the family name of the Duke of Westminster, multi-millionaire landlord of the Belgravia area north of Victoria.) In the 1990s, as with other London railway termini, the value of the space above the platforms has been realised with the huge Victoria Plaza complex of shops, restaurants and offices. Whether Senior Service still satisfy cannot be told, since the building carrying the advert in Terminus Place and the trees in Grosvenor Gardens are obscured by more of the 'glass building-block' development (housing the headquarters of the John Lewis Partnership) along the south side of Victoria Street. The cluster of buildings on the right horizon of the 1960 view are the Victoria & Albert Museum, the dome of Brompton Oratory and the tower of Imperial College, over a mile and a half away. Finally, as a detail, note how the roof of the building in the centre foreground has been transformed by the addition of ducts and fans, presumably in connection with that modern luxury, office air-conditioning! *C. F. B. Penley, A. Mott collection/WA*

Swinging the camera slightly to the right, and looking almost directly westwards, we are now back where we started. On the left, beside the Senior Service advert, is the very top of Victoria Street, at its junction with Buckingham Palace Road. The building on the right of the street with the domed tower is the Victoria Palace Theatre, built as a music-hall in 1911. It was the home of the Crazy Gang from 1947 to 1962, then the Black & White Minstrels, who gave almost 4,500 performances until 1970. While the gardens of Buckingham Palace, bordered by Grosvenor Place, can be seen in the top right-hand

corner of the 1960 view, today the whole of the north side of Victoria Street and beyond has been redeveloped. Esso House is going up on the right, joined in the 1996 view (extreme right) by the 334-foot Portland Tower. The contrast between the flat roofs, chimney pots (what few remain in 1960!) and severe-looking brick rears of the earlier Victoria Street buildings and the delicate glazed blocks that have replaced them is fascinating, and epitomises London 'past' and London 'present'! *C. F. B. Penley, A. Mott collection/WA*

9. THE WEST END

Apsley House, the tall colonnaded building facing **HYDE PARK CORNER**, had the distinction in the early days of the post office of being known as 'No 1 London'. It certainly had a distinguished occupant, having been bought by the nation in 1820 for the Duke of Wellington in acknowledgement of his services. In the 1996 view his statue can be seen astride his faithful mount Copenhagen, who carried him at Waterloo, looking at his home from the island. Although 50 years ago the junction was not as forbidding an interchange as it is now, it could still be referred to in 1940 as 'one of the world's busiest traffic centres. Vehicular traffic passes the "Corner" on the gyratory system. A recent census shows that some 83,000 vehicles pass this point between 8 am and 8 pm - or nearly a hundred a minute.' A census in 1995 showed an average of 43,000 vehicles in 12 hours, a sizeable reduction.

Not much is passing on this day in March 1957, but that is explained by petrol rationing in the wake of the Suez Crisis, which erupted in July 1956. To the left of Apsley House is the 'screen' forming the ceremonial entrance to Hyde Park from Buckingham Palace via Constitution Hill, and to the right is the town house built for Lord Rothschild in 1862. At this date Park Lane was only a narrow road, entering Piccadilly off to the right of the picture.

Then in 1961-2 Park Lane became a dual carriageway, was slewed to the west, the first few houses on the north of Piccadilly were demolished, and the new wide road entered Hyde Park Corner next to Apsley House, more or less where the No 16 bus is on the right of the 1957 photo (and to the right of the white lorry in 1996). The house, which today contains the Wellington Museum, was left rather marooned, and its newly exposed east side had to be re-faced. At the same time an underpass between Piccadilly and Knightsbridge was constructed to allow straight-through traffic to avoid the Corner, and the eastern entrance to this can be seen in the 1996 view; a labyrinth of subways connects the various roads and allows pedestrian access to the island. On the right is now the modern Hotel InterContinental, while in the distance can be seen the 1966 270-foot tower of Knightsbridge Barracks. *London Transport Museum/WA*

Following the road improvements, this is the eastern side of **HYDE PARK CORNER** on Wednesday 13 May 1964, with traffic from Piccadilly (right) merging with that circulating from the north side. The Routemaster bus is advertising Sheepdog Trials in Hyde Park over the Whitsun weekend, and coach-air fares to Paris apparently for £9! It can be seen that some of the older houses in Piccadilly survived, together with those on the east side of Hamilton Place, which was cut through in the 1860s to relieve the traffic bottleneck at the south end of the old Park Lane (off the picture to the right). The photograph is dominated by the newly completed Hilton Hotel in Park Lane, opened in 1963. It has 30 floors and over 500 bedrooms, with a rooftop restaurant and bar, one of the earliest in London.

By 1996 the buildings on the left have long gone, to be replaced by the Hotel InterContinental, which opened in September 1975, but some of those in Hamilton Place have survived, now overshadowed by the Londonderry House Hotel of 1964-9. One thing hasn't changed, and that is the continued use of the venerable Routemaster buses. The post-deregulation example here has reverted to the name 'London General', which was carried by many London buses from the mid-19th century until the formation of the London Passenger Transport Board in 1933. Road markings now aid the circulation round this complex interchange, while trees along Piccadilly and on the Hyde Park Corner island help to soften today's view. *London Transport Museum/WA*

A few years later, and the new **PARK LANE** is fully established. Originally it was literally just a lane outside the high brick wall that enclosed Hyde Park (off to the left in these views). In the 18th century a few houses began to appear along the east side, but it was not until the 1820s that it became a sought-after address. By the late 1930s Arthur Mee could write that the road was 'passing through a great transformation. A few of its old houses are still left but the old charm has passed away and vast hotels on the American scale have banished all remembrance of the days when this was one of the enjoyable walks in London.'

Yet greater change occurred at the beginning of the 1960s when it became a six-lane dual carriageway with a broad, leafy, but largely inaccessible central reservation, swallowing up a sizeable portion of Hyde Park. This 18 July 1969 view shows the southbound carriageway at the bottom end; originally Park Lane continued off to the right on the line of the old houses. The characteristic late 18th/early 19th century bow-window designs were originally the *rears* of the houses whose fronts are in Curzon Place, their back gardens once adjoining the park. Since being 'turned round', several of the bows have been modernised with almost full glazing. The modern building on the left on the corner of Curzon Street was built in 1963-5 for the Playboy Club (the first, complete with 'bunny-girls', was opened by Hugh Heffner in Chicago in 1960). On the extreme right can be seen the front of the Hilton Hotel. In 1996 we managed to catch a slightly quieter scene, and the No 16 bus approaching the extended bus lane is a modern rear-engined Metrobus. *London Transport Museum/WA*

MARBLE ARCH was designed by John Nash in 1828 as the gateway to Buckingham Palace (see pages 124-5), but it had to be moved when the new east front of the Palace was built; it was subsequently re-erected in 1851 at the top of Park Lane at its junction with Oxford Street, Edgware Road and Bayswater Road. It became the centre of a traffic island in 1908 and, if the 1940 Red Guide is to be believed, before the war saw 60,000 vehicles between 8 am and 8 pm; by 1995 only about 27,000 were recorded in a 12-hour census (of which only about 1,800 were heavy goods vehicles) - as with Hyde Park Corner, a substantial and welcome reduction.

In June 1952 a fine Coventry-registered Standard Vanguard 'Beetleback' and a trio of buses pass close to the south side of the Arch, in an area formerly separated from the road by railings. By 1997 it can be seen that the road has been pushed back further, leaving pleasant gardens around the Arch. The position of the present road is shown in the third view; the 36 bus route is catered for by an RT in 1952 and an elderly Routemaster in 1997. This wider view allows a glimpse of the massive Cumberland Hotel above the Arch - this was built in 1933 and has nearly 900 bedrooms. *London Transport Museum/WA (2)*

Opposite page We now move into **OXFORD STREET**, which originally formed part of an old Roman way from Hampshire to Suffolk, and the more modern route between the heart of the City at Bank and Shepherds Bush in West London, thence to Oxford. Its name was established in the early 18th century when land to the north was coincidentally acquired by the Earl of Oxford - on a map of 1724 it was referred to as 'Oxford Street, the Road to Oxford'. Originally residential, by the end of the last century it was beginning to take on its modern guise with an influx of drapers and department stores. A post-war shopping guide for visitors describes the street as 'emphatically cosmopolitan in character; indeed, one may walk through it and emerge on the other side without having heard a single word of English spoken', which is of course still very much true today! So sought-after by retailers did it become that in the late 1930s space was rated at £30 a square foot.

There's not much of a gay, cosmopolitan air in this October 1949 photograph looking east from outside D. H. Evans's - it simply oozes post-war austerity! The wide, unattractive-looking street has a curious surface of what appears to be a brick-like paving, with metallic grips near the pavements - to aid horses' adhesion, perhaps? On the right a rag, waste paper and metal merchant's lorry is passing a parked railway delivery van that still carries its pre-nationalisation (1948) 'GWR' roundel and an advert for Torox beef cubes. On the first floor behind, 'Teen Togs' are being advertised - teenagers had probably only just been invented! The No 13 bus is advertising *Woman's Own* (first published in 1932), the one behind 'Wisk - does the big wash'.

In 1996 Oxford Street really does live up to its name as the capital's premier shopping street. Traffic - taxis and buses only - have been squeezed into the middle to allow for wider, more 'strollable' pavements, with stylish lamp standards carrying banners encouraging the wrapping and binning of chewing-gum (a major pavement-disfiguring problem today - those teenagers again!) and young trees. Most of the buildings on the south side survive.

In August 1996 bus shelters in Oxford Street were in the news when an advertising agency dreamed up the idea of marketing a new soft drink by installing infra-red sensors in ten bus shelter billboards; these detected the presence of a queue and released a spray of 'the flavour of a lemon orchard'. One wonders what the stern-faced overcoated 1949 shoppers would have made of such frivolity. . . *London Transport Museum/WA*

This page The Christmas shopping rush is well under way outside Selfridges in **OXFORD STREET** on Monday 8 December 1958 ('14 more shopping days' advises the notice on the window). The relatively narrow pavements are crammed with shoppers, many glancing at Selfridge's famous Christmas window decorations.

Gordon Selfridge opened his first store in Chicago in 1902, but

sold up and came to Europe. Built in 1908-9, nothing like his colossal Oxford Street store, with its 500-foot frontage, had been seen in England before. The post-war shopping guide advises that, 'In this immense store there are over 200 different departments, and between them they cater for every imaginable need of civilised man. . .' ('from parasols to pineapples' as the 1940 *Red Guide* puts it). Arthur Mee describes how people smiled when Selfridge set up his great shop 'at the wrong end of Oxford Street where nobody came. People come today in their thousands and hundreds of thousands, and all the world knows Selfridge's. . .'

To compare December 1958 with May 1996 is perhaps not quite 'like for like', but Selfridge's is still one of the great Oxford Street stores. It now faces on to a wider, leafier pavement with benches for the weary shopper, the result of improvements completed in November 1993. The comparison of four decades of fashions is instructive! *London Transport Museum/WA*

This page **NEW BOND STREET** was laid out in the 1720s by the Earl of Oxford as the northern continuation of (Old) Bond Street, named after Sir Thomas Bond, who owned the land in the 17th century. Ever an exclusive shopping street, after the war it was famous for jewellers, art galleries, auctioneers, tailors and couturiers. This is no less so today, although many of the names have changed with the fashions. The past view, looking from the corner of Brook Street up towards Oxford Street, was taken at 4.45 pm on Saturday 6 October 1962, when Bond Street was open to two-way traffic; the Daimler, 4 DYR, perhaps contains a wealthy customer. Old Bond Street was even narrower than this, perhaps the narrowest of London's important streets and a notorious bottleneck.

Today it is one-way southbound, with three lanes of cars bearing down on the unwary shopper. Bennett's camera shop still sells photographic equipment under the Dixon's name, while Bentley the jeweller has become a shop for 'designer label' Guy Laroche. Hunt's (and upstairs the Lucie Clayton Model School) is now Escada, and beyond there are two furriers, at a time when such things were less frowned upon; the lady on the corner in the foreground sports an expensive-looking fur jacket, and clutches handbag, gloves and a neatly covered umbrella (perhaps she won 'more on Copes', as the bus advises us!). Further up there is one of Carwardine's restaurants for tea and coffee.

The 'past' photograph was taken from the first floor of what is now an Armani shop - your photographer, in baggy-kneed jeans and charity shop jacket, felt that a pavement-level shot would do the job perfectly adequately. . . *London Transport Museum/WA*

Opposite page **OXFORD CIRCUS** forms the intersection of Oxford Street and Regent Street. The four quadrants are of identical design and date from between 1913 and 1928 - one was heavily bombed during the war but was repaired. This 'past' view was taken from the first floor of Peter Robinson's store looking west along Oxford Street between 9.30 and 10.00 am on Thursday 23 September 1954. As the postwar shopping guide tells us, 'furs strike the dominant note and fill the windows - on the northern side is Swears & Wells, and in the other corner, Jays, renowned also as a dressmaker.' (The fourth corner was occupied by Spirella corsets.) Yorkshireman Peter Robinson opened his first shop on this site in 1833; part of the Burton Group since 1946, today it carries the name Top Shop. Real furs have now, of course, gone; on the left is now Benetton, on the right Hennes & Mauritz.

Familiar names like Saxone and Salisbury's can be seen in the 1954 photograph, as well as period detail such as a shop selling 'gowns and mantles'; there's also a branch of the 'Fifty Shilling Tailor'. The buses are advertising the *News of the World* ('War-time secrets that can now be told'), Weston's biscuits, and *This is Cinerama*, the first Cinerama film, released in 1952 and showing at the London Casino (now the Prince Edward Theatre). The cobbled paving of the Circus can be seen, together with minimum traffic control and no pedestrian protection.

The 1996 view (which could not be taken from upstairs) shows that while the buildings still maintain the 'Circus' shape, the originally concave segments of the pavement have become convex, protected by stout balustrades, making the road more of a conventional crossroads in shape and allowing space for entrances to the subways and underground station. The walls also provide an ideal place to sit, to see and be seen! No motor vehicles except buses and taxis are allowed in Oxford Street today, and the pedestrian crossing has lights and protective barriers on the central refuge. *London Transport Museum/WA*

Here is another aerial view that unfortunately could not be exactly replicated, looking from Oxford Circus southwards down **REGENT STREET**. Dated April 1955, it shows such a wealth of period vehicles that it seemed a pity not to include it! Amongst them is a lorry carrying sacks of coal (not much demand for that in central London today!), a Scammell 'mechanical horse' three-wheeled British Railways delivery dray, and a wide variety of cars and vans, every one of which would today make a vintage vehicle collector's mouth water! The shops include Spirella corsets on the extreme left, then Helen Kaye ladies' fashions, London Shoe, Dr Scholl's and a branch of the National Provincial Bank (in 1968 becoming a constituent of the NatWest). Then follows Dickins & Jones store, established in Oxford Street in 1790 and still a feature of Regent Street today.

Regent Street was part of John Nash's grand design for a *Via Triumphalis* (Triumphal Way, or 'New Street', as it was originally referred to) from Carlton House to Regent's Park. It was cut through amidst much upheaval in the early 18th century, but by the 1920s had been almost entirely rebuilt, leaving us the street as we know it today.

It is impossible to read the newspaper hoarding held by the white-coated vendor outside Jay's in 1955, but in 1996 the *Evening Standard* is leading with a story about footballer 'Gazza' (Paul Gascoigne). The new entrance to Oxford Circus underground station reminds us that this is not just an important junction above ground; beneath the Circus is the interchange between the Central Line (running beneath Oxford Street and opened in 1900), the Bakerloo Line (running north-south beneath Regent Street and opened in 1906) and the Victoria Line (which opened in 1969 and to accommodate which the station was rebuilt). *London Transport Museum/WA*

One of London's most famous variety theatres, the **PALLADIUM** is tucked away behind Oxford Circus in Argyll Street. It opened in 1910 as a luxurious music-hall, and became officially known as the London Palladium in 1934. It is perhaps best remembered as the venue for the live one-hour TV show *Sunday Night at the London Palladium*, which was a weekly event from 1954 to 1965, and was revived less successfully in the early 1970s. Comperes included Tommy Trinder, Bruce Forsyth, Norman Vaughan and Jim Dale. TV critic Philip Purser described it in 1959 as 'one of life's reassuring certainties. Cheery compère will succeed high-stepping girls; "Beat the Clock" will follow a couple of lesser turns; finally there will be the Big Star, and all the lush splendour of the revolving-stage finale.'

From Saturday 4 October 1980, according to the 'past' photograph, the theatre is presenting American entertainer Lynda Carter, who had enjoyed success on television in the late 1970s as 'Wonder Woman'. Forthcoming attractions include 'Britain's foremost entertainer', Max Bygraves, and the Four Tops, the 1960s Motown chartbusters who in 1981 were to experience a revival of fortunes with their first UK Top 3 hit in ten years.

Jim Dale returned to the Palladium in 1994, receiving critical acclaim as Fagin in a revival of Lionel Bart's famous musical *Oliver!*, first performed in London at the Albery Theatre, St Martin's Lane, from 1960 to 1966 in a record run of 2,618 performances; it was revived again in 1977.

The Palladium is currently owned by Stoll Moss Holdings; as can be seen from the van delivering potted plants, that company is also the proprietor of the Queen's, Gielgud, Apollo, Lyric, Her Majesty's, Garrick, Cambridge, Theatre Royal, Royalty and Duchess theatres. It was announced in September 1996 that multimillionaire musical producer Cameron Mackintosh, who is responsible for *Oliver!*, might be about to bid for seven other West End theatres currently owned by Mayfair Theatres & Cinemas - the Piccadilly, Comedy, Wyndham's, Albery, Phoenix, Whitehall and Donmar Warehouse (he already owns the Prince of Wales and Prince Edward). It was felt that the West End would benefit from so many theatres being owned by someone who actually puts on productions. *C. Mott, A. Mott collection/WA*

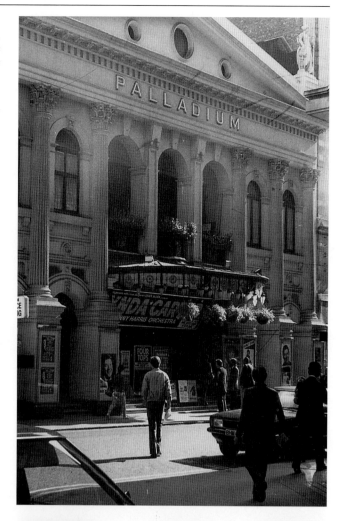

Opposite page As originally envisaged by Nash in 1819, **PICCADILLY CIRCUS** was indeed a Circus, formed by the crossroads of Regent Street and Piccadilly. However, in the 1880s the north-east corner, seen here in this view from the late 1950s (Disney's *Old Yeller* - advertised on the left - was released in 1957, and the Guinness clock, under scaffolding, was replaced in 1959), was destroyed to make way for Shaftesbury Avenue, and thereafter the Circus was more of an awkward triangle. Moreover, at the turn of the century the retailers on the northern side discovered the advantages of bright electric advertising hoardings, and the Bovril and Schweppes signs, erected in 1910, were a familiar feature of the corner of Shaftesbury Avenue for many years. On the opposite corner the new London Pavilion followed suit, soon becoming smothered in signs. On the south side of the Circus the Crown was landlord, and such advertising was *not* allowed.

The scene in 1996 shows many changes. Gone are Bovril and Schweppes, to be replaced by assorted Australian, American and Japanese products - not a British name among them! Gone too are the famous Guinness clocks (see overleaf). The Pavilion has been shorn of all its advertisements (for gin, disinfectant, chewing-gum, razors, petrol) and looks the better for it, newly restored and painted. The 1957 'do it yourself' road layout, with minimal markings and signs, was to change completely with the remodelling of the Circus in the 1980s.

A plan was unveiled in 1972 for the complete redevelopment of the Pavilion and Criterion sites, with towers linked by pedestrian decks. However, in the event the biggest change involved the famous statue of Eros being relocated to what is in effect a 'peninsula' rather than an 'island'! It was removed in 1985, returning in March

1986. Two years later, after restoration work, the statue and its fountain base, now moved some yards to the east, were unveiled once more. No longer having any pretensions of being a Circus, traffic now moves eastbound only round the top of the area. It certainly makes public access to the statue easier, as the steps around the base have always been a popular place to sit and watch the world go by. The new position is evident in the 1996 view, with traffic converging from Piccadilly (left) and Lower Regent Street (right). *N. L. Browne, courtesy of Frank Hornby/WA*

This page This second view of **PICCADILLY CIRCUS** on an unknown date in the 1950s shows clearly how effectively the London Pavilion has been restored - and how Eros has been shifted out of the picture altogether to its peninsula on the right! Built in 1885, the Pavilion was once a music hall and subsequently a theatre. Between 1934 and 1978 it was a cinema; later the inside was remodelled within the original facade, to be re-opened in 1988 by Margaret Thatcher. Its principal feature is now 'Rock Circus', 'Britain's No 1 Rock Attraction', complete with effigies of famous rock stars on the balconies. With such attractions as Alton Towers and Warwick Castle, it is part of The Tussauds Group, a far cry

from when Marie Tussaud arrived in England from France in 1802 with 35 wax figures inherited from her uncle! It is described thus: 'Audio-animatronic moving and static wax figures, lasers, authentic memorabilia, videos, archive film and personal stereo sound surround you and astound you. . .' Like all great tourist venues, London has always used cutting-edge technology to attract visitors, and in its way Rock Circus is a direct descendent of Barker's remarkable 90-foot-diameter Panorama built 200 years earlier a few hundred yards away in Leicester Square.

As in the Circus itself, the advertisements on the corner of Haymarket in the right background have been reduced from Pan Yan pickle, Osram light-bulbs and BOAC to a single one for Hitachi.

The famous statue itself, the first in London to be made from aluminium and dating from 1892, was intended to symbolise the Angel of Christian Charity rather than Eros the God of Love. It was erected by public subscription in memory of the reformer and philanthropist the 7th Earl of Shaftesbury. Since 1937 it has been boarded up to prevent invasion by New Year revellers, and during the war, from 1939 to 1948, it was kept in Egham, Surrey. *A. J. Pike, courtesy of Frank Hornby/WA*

Whether or not the illuminated advertisements in **PICCADILLY CIRCUS** are considered an eyesore, they have certainly provided London with one of its most famous nightly attractions. These three views are of the corner of Piccadilly Circus/Glasshouse Street and Shaftesbury Avenue. The first, taken at 9.35 pm on 24 June 1954, shows a Coca-Cola advert under erection between one for Ever Ready batteries and one of the famous Guinness clocks, complete with seals. These illuminated clocks were once a feature of many major cities, including Brighton, Bristol, Cardiff and Newcastle, and were derived from a famous poster of a clock face used to advertise Guinness. The first appeared in Piccadilly Circus in 1932; after a break during the war from 1939 to 1949, they were remodelled in 1954 and 1959.

Some time after the latter year, the second view shows a Double Diamond ad erected above the Coca-Cola one, and Forte's have opened a restaurant below. The new Guinness clock surmounts an ad for Morley nylons, while Bovril and Schweppes still dominate the corner.

In 1996 the Saqui & Lawrence jewellers shop is now H. Samuel, the Guinness clock is gone and Coca-Cola has been squeezed up by McDonald's. The humble Ever Ready battery has been superseded by Japanese TV, video and fax; magnetic videotape was just beginning to be used in television recording in the 1950s, the first video recorder having been demonstrated in 1952, while fax was not widely available until the 1980s. A Burger King restaurant has replaced Forte's. *C. F. B. Penley, A. Mott collection/F. C. Le Manquais, courtesy of Tom Middlemass/WA*

The Criterion Theatre stands on the south side of **PICCADILLY CIRCUS**, and the 'past' view, from about 1980, clearly shows the roadway on the south side of the island and relatively narrow pavement, now replaced by the broad 'peninsula' on which Eros stands, allowing space for an extra entrance to the underground station and pedestrian 'circus' (see overleaf).

The Criterion started life as the basement concert hall annex to the Criterion Restaurant, built in the 1870s, and was one of the first theatres to be constructed entirely underground. By the early 1980s the restaurant was empty, but recent redevelopment work has seen it re-open, with what appears to be a new entrance cut through to Lillywhite's famous sports store, where once was Trusthouse Forte's offices. Established by the son of 19th-century

Sussex cricketer Frederick Lillywhite, the UK's largest sports shop has been on this site since 1925. The 'present' picture is neatly fixed in time by the banner announcing Euro 96.

The Criterion Theatre has a long tradition of comedy; in the 'past' photograph the show is *Tomfoolery*, featuring the words and music of American songwriter Tom Lehrer, whose satirical songs about drugs and atomic warfare made him one of the popular voices of the 1960s. The show was compiled by and starred Robin Ray, and featured perhaps Lehrer's best-known song, 'Poisoning pigeons in the park' (see page 100!). The 1996 hit is the 'Reduced Shakespeare Company' in *The Complete Works of William Shakespeare (abridged)* - the whole of the Bard in a single evening! *C. Mott, A. Mott collection/WA*

The Baker Street & Waterloo Railway (soon to be reduced to 'Bakerloo Line') was the first underground railway to cross central London from north to south, and opened in 1906. The same year the Piccadilly Line opened, and the two crossed at **PICCADILLY CIRCUS UNDERGROUND STATION**. In 1907 1.5 million people used the station, but by 1922 this had grown to a staggering 18 million (or some 49,000 people a day - a recent one-day survey gives today's figure as still over 44,000). The station was therefore rebuilt in 1924-8 with the entire booking hall underground. The Eros statue was temporarily removed to County Hall (and not replaced until the end of 1933) and the shaft to the works below sunk in its place. The new circulating area was not quite circular (having a diameter of between 144 and 155 feet), and the roadway above was supported on a 'spider's web' of steel girders and joists, amazingly with minimum disruption to traffic. Today the station still contains many of the design features of that rebuilding, as seen in the 'past' view dated 24 June 1959. The columns supporting the ceiling were of imitation stone with narrow brass fillets at the angles and twin lampshades at the top (removed in the 1959 shot, but since replaced). Set in the outer wall were stairways to the various street exits, basement shop windows for Swan & Edgar's department store (a famous Piccadilly Circus landmark until its closure in 1982), booking office, telephone booths and 26 automatic electric ticket machines. A couple of these are seen in the 1959 view, each issuing tickets to one fare value only. The pre-decimalisation fare and list of corresponding destinations is shown on the illuminated panel, with slots below for silver sixpence or one shilling coins, or 'coppers' (threepenny bits, pennies and halfpennies); presumably the machines were able to calculate and dispense change.

The minimum 3d fare in 1959 was £1.10 in 1996, 88 times greater!

Modern-day electronics enable much more compact ticket machines; destination and type of ticket can be selected by the customer and an illuminated display shows the fare. Payment can be made by coin, banknote or even credit card; change is nearly always available. The tickets carry magnetic bands and are passed through automatic ticket barriers, which cancel them on exit to prevent a single-journey ticket being use more than once. Because flash photography is not permitted anywhere on the underground, the modern ticket machines seen here are those at Westminster station, at street level and open to daylight. *London Transport Museum/WA*

A cut-away view from the 1940s showing the complex of tunnels and escalators at Piccadilly Circus. *R. Macpherson, from Odhams's Railways, Ships and Planes*

Lifts, escalators and stairs connected the booking area to the platforms. Shown here, possibly during the 1950s, is the northbound Bakerloo Line platform at **PICCADILLY CIRCUS UNDERGROUND STATION**. A Watford-bound train has just arrived, and passengers are alighting from a No Smoking carriage. Today, since the catastrophic fire at King's Cross underground station in 1987, smoking is banned on the whole of the underground system. At the end of the train can be seen the standard 'tube' tunnel ('tube' because they were bored though the ground and lined to a circular section, rather than the earlier sub-surface 'cut-and-cover' tunnels, which were of square section). The tube tunnels have a diameter of between 11 ft 8 in and 12 ft 6 in, while the station tunnels are just over 21 feet in diameter, accommodating on the Bakerloo a 291-foot-long platform. Originally, as seen here, the ceilings were plastered and

whitewashed, broken with rings of tiles whose colours differed between stations so that regular users could more easily identify their destination.

Over recent decades the formerly rather gloomy aspect of the tube stations has been enhanced with lively decoration appropriate to each station, together with much improved lighting, both along the centre of the roof and concealed along the walls. A good example is Charing Cross station, also on the Bakerloo Line, seen here in the 'present' photograph. Details from works in the nearby National Gallery and National Portrait Gallery decorate the walls, while the new-style 'Next train' indicator not only shows the order of approaching trains, but also counts down the time in minutes before arrival, as well as being able to display other messages. So brightly lit are today's stations that this picture was able to be taken without the use of a flash. *London Transport Museum/WA*

Opposite page The origin of the name **PICCADILLY** has never been established with certainty. It may be connected with a 'piccadill', a kind of stiff collar fashionable at the beginning of the 17th century; one supplier made his fortune from them and built himself a house in the area, nick-named Piccadilly Hall. Alternatively, it may come from the Dutch word 'pikedillekens', meaning scraps or corners of a piece of cloth, this area then being the tip or corner of built-up London.

Whatever, by the middle of the 18th century this ancient thoroughfare (with Oxford Street one of the old routes west-ward from the City) was built upon as far as Hyde Park Corner. Since then the resi-dential nature of the street has become a sought-after address for commercial offices and hotels, and virtually all the buildings are post-1860. On the right here at the eastern (Piccadilly Circus) end in October 1949 is the Piccadilly Hotel with its traditional coating of London soot (now cleaned as Le Meridien); built in 1905-8, its frontage recedes behind a screen of giant columns (today the loca-tion of the glazed Terrace restaurant). The buildings beyond are in the course of demolition in 1949, and have since been replaced by modern offices, but still nice-ly in scale with the rest of the street. On the left in the 'present' view can be seen Simpson's famous store, built in 1935-6, the first welded steel building in London.

The broad unmarked roadway of 1949 features a queue of cars and taxis very much from the 'any colour you like as long as it's black' era, together with buses advertising 'Zesto Pickle', Swan Vestas and Borwick's baking-powder (the last two still very much with us in the 1990s). Adamson's Bedford lorry looks new. For some years Piccadilly has been one-way at the eastern end, although a 'contraflow' bus lane accommodates westbound buses. To avoid confusing unwary pedes-trians, this is well marked and protected by substantial refuges with traffic lights. *London Transport Museum/WA*

This page **LOWER REGENT STREET** was a continuation of Nash's 'New Street' designed to link Regent's Park with Carlton House in Pall Mall. To avoid cutting into the fashion-able St James's area south of Piccadilly, and to allow Regent Street to intersect with the east end of Pall Mall, (upper) Regent Street

turned east to enter the side of Piccadilly Circus in front of the County Fire Office (at the top of the street in both of these views), then continued south-eastwards to Waterloo Place in Pall Mall.

Hardly anything has changed in the 43 years separating these two photographs, the 'past' one having been taken at 1.40 pm on Saturday 12 September 1953. On the left, with the dome, is the Plaza cinema (today the UCI Plaza), showing the famous Alan Ladd western *Shane*, then on release. In 1996 one of the four Plaza screens is showing the movie version of *Mission Impossible*, which

ran on TV from 1966 to 1972. It stars Tom Cruise, who was two years old when Ladd died in 1964.

Even in 1953 the road was one-way northbound, but there are no controlled pedestrian crossings as a bowler-hatted busi-nessman crosses in the foreground, with a London 'bobby' strolling towards a road-sweeper's hand-cart further up. Today there are controlled crossings, and road markings are more explicit. There's an interesting comparison of taxi designs on the left. *C. F. B. Penley, A. Mott collection/WA*

Parallel with Lower Regent Street, heading down from the east side of Piccadilly Circus, is **HAYMARKET**; in the 17th century the Royal Mews were nearby towards present-day Trafalgar Square, so hay and straw would have been in demand. This road is one-way southbound, as the sign on the lamp standard to the right of the October 1953 'past' photograph tells us. Halfway down is what was originally the Carlton Theatre of 1926; converted to a cinema in 1929, it was sold to Paramount in 1930, and is now owned by MGM, with three screens. Parked outside in 1953 is a sleek Armstrong Siddeley.

The 1953 presentation is *The Man Between*, described by film historian Leslie Halliwell as an 'imitation *Third Man* [which Reed had also directed, in 1949] with an uninteresting mystery and a solemn ending. Good acting and production can't save it.' The same year James Mason had played Brutus in *Julius Caesar* with John Gielgud and Marlon Brando, while *The Man Between* was only the fourth film of 22-year-old Claire Bloom. The more graphic advertising of the film is in contrast to the 1990s style of illuminated panel with titles only. Also by contrast is the nature and tone of today's films: *Trainspotting* (18), a tale of Edinburgh drug addicts described by the film magazine *Empire* as 'the best British film of the decade . . . dark and dirty, violent and mean, but . . also violently affecting. . .'; *Things To Do In Denver When You're Dead* (18) (starring Andy Garcia, not born until 1956), a quirky crime film; and

Kids (also 18), 'a loose semi-documentary about New York's teen youth'. Despite being the story of a West Berlin racketeer and double agent whose death arises from his love for Claire Bloom, *The Man Between* still rates a U certificate - one can imagine that the treatment today would certainly bring it into the 15 or 18 category. . . *C. F. B. Penley, A. Mott collection/WA*

Below A Carlton presentation back in 1950 was Billy Wilder's celebrated *Sunset Boulevard* starring William Holden and Gloria Swanson. Two-year-old Andrew Lloyd Webber won't have been aware of it then, but in the 1990s he turned it into an award-winning stage musical starring Petula Clark (now, unbelievably, in her 60s, and older than Gloria Swanson was in 1950!).

The **WINDMILL THEATRE** was a London theatrical institution. Named after its location in Great Windmill Street (off Shaftesbury Avenue), itself named after a windmill that stood here until the late 18th century, it was built in 1910 as a cinema, the Palais de Luxe. It became a theatre in 1931, and the following year general manager Vivian Van Damm introduced his 'Revudeville', a non-stop variety show that ran from 2.30 to 11 pm every day, and was famous for its nearly-nude tableaux (the girls were required by law to remain motionless). 'Any additional artificial aid to vision is NOT permitted,' warns a 1949 programme. 'All scenes presented at this Theatre are fully protected and must not be photographed or reproduced. . .' As it was a continuous performance, the management reserved the right to re-sell any seat left vacant for more than 15 minutes. Apart from a couple of weeks in 1939, the Windmill was the only theatre in London to stay open during the Second World War, hence its proud 'We Never Closed' slogan.

Van Damm died in 1960, and his daughter ran the theatre until 1964, when it finally did close and reverted to a cinema. In 1973 it was acquired by Paul Raymond, who returned it to its former - and by this time more explicit - role. In this guise it is seen here in about 1980, presenting *Rip Off!*, 'Live on stage . . . full frontal sexual exposure . . . the erotic experience of the era'. But by 1981 it was closed again, and since then has had a chequered history as a theatre restaurant until 1986, thereafter the Paramount City Theatre, again for nude shows and variety, and currently as a discotheque under the same name.

A row of the familiar red telephone boxes can be seen on the right in both pictures. Their survival in the 1990s is the subject of heated debate. English Heritage warned of 'visual chaos' as less than ideal new BT designs and those of rival companies proliferate; in 1996 it organised a meeting between the phone companies and the Royal Fine Art Commission to suggest a competition to come up with a worthy successor to architect George Gilbert Scott's classic 'K6' design. Meanwhile, Westminster City Council has decreed that the familiar red box must be retained in historic locations. *C. Mott, A. Mott collection/WA*

Below As well as its nudes, the stage of the Windmill Theatre was famous as the nursery of several well-known entertainers. Harry Secombe appeared there after his demob in 1946, and Jimmy Edwards made his stage debut there in the same year; Tony Hancock was another. This 1949 programme has newcomer Arthur English (no doubt in his famous 'Spiv' role, and later of *Are You Being Served?* fame on TV), and features 21-year-old Bruce Forsythe (then with an 'e') in various supporting roles. He had left school in 1932 at the age of 14 and worked as 'Boy Bruce, the Mighty Atom'. He appeared at the Windmill from 1945 to 1951, with a two-year break for RAF service. Then in 1958 he was 'discovered' and invited to compere *Sunday Night At The London Palladium. Authors' collection*

Left and below left Many of the photographs in this book were taken by Charles Penley, who during the 1950s and 1960s was manager of the **EMPIRE CINEMA, LEICESTER SQUARE.** Born in 1894, he was the son of W. S. Penley, who played the original title role in *Charley's Aunt* (and may have been Brandon Thomas's co-author). Before taking over at the Empire Charles Penley was a theatrical producer, putting on many shows. Some of his many photographs of the Empire are shown here.

The land in this area was acquired in the 17th century by the 2nd Earl of Leicester, who built Leicester House on what is now the north side of the Square; one of the largest houses in London, it was demolished in the 1790s. During the 19th century the Square began to take on the character familiar today, as a general centre of entertainment.

To compare a snowy Tuesday 2 March 1954 with a sunny May day in 1996 is not really fair, but it is clear that the gardens have changed quite a bit. They were originally Lammas land, available free to parishioners for drying clothes and pasturing cattle after Lammas Day (12 August). For many years until the last century they were criticised for their dilapidated state, until bought for the public in 1874 and laid out with the fountain and statue of Shakespeare in the centre, and busts of other great men who had once lived in the Square. Over a century later a delightful statue of Charlie Chaplin was added (unveiled by Sir Ralph Richardson in 1981). Even since the war Leicester Square has been described as 'the dullest of all our famous squares', and was in recent times a haunt of vagrants and 'winos', but at long last has been refurbished, being re-opened by the Queen in June 1992.

The Empire Cinema itself opened in 1928 on the site of the Royal London Panorama; in 1884 this was rebuilt as the Empire Theatre, which became a music-hall in 1887 and was pulled down in 1927. In 1954 the main feature is *Kiss Me Kate*, starring Howard Keel and Kathryn Grayson; this was the 3-D screen version of the Broadway hit based on Shakespeare's *The Taming of the Shrew*. There's 'real' Shakespeare next door at the Ritz in the form of *Julius Caesar* (already referred to on page 154). On the right is the Monseigneur News Theatre; these were once popular in London as a continuous programme of news and cartoons in the days before almost universal television ownership. *C. F. B. Penley, A. Mott collection/WA*

Left This Thursday 3 September 1953 view was taken to record the première week of the Roman epic *Quo Vadis* (complete with centurions on the pavement outside!) on 'the new giant panoramic screen'. MGM claimed to be 'privileged to add something of permanent value to the cultural treasure house of mankind', but despite a distinguished cast that included Robert Taylor, Deborah Kerr and Peter Ustinov (in an Oscar-nominated role as Nero), film historian Leslie Halliwell considered it 'three hours of solemn tedium with flashes of vigorous acting and a few set pieces to take the eye.' On the far corner is another 1950s phenomenon - a milk bar! *C. F. B. Penley, A. Mott collection*

This page The first two views, looking in the opposite direction, also show the north side of Leicester Square when traffic circulated around it. The first, dated 1953, shows the feature presentation to be *Lili*, a 'romantic whimsy' starring Leslie Caron and Mel Ferrer. Note the MGM lion above the main hoarding.

The second view was taken on the wet evening of Sunday 16 December 1956, and is an atmospheric and nostalgic reminder of when queuing for the 'one and nines' along the pavement under umbrellas was a national pastime! The film is *High Society*, with Grace Kelly, Bing Crosby and Frank Sinatra (a musical reworking by Cole Porter of the much better *Philadelphia Story* of 1940, starring Katharine Hepburn and Cary Grant). On the left is the Dolcis building of 1937, in the 'anonymous modern idiom, just with band upon band stream-lined round a rounded corner' (Pevsner). In the right background can be seen the Warner cinema of 1938 ('wildly modernistic') and beyond that the Hippodrome, later the Talk of the Town (see also page 103).

The 1996 view shows the now pedestrianised Square. The Empire's modern canopy is rather garish, but the removal of the hoarding has revealed the dramatic 1920s picture-house architecture behind. *C. F. B. Penley, A. Mott collection (2)/WA*

Below Warner Leicester Square presentations, 1950: *Colt .45* starring Western stalwart Randolph Scott (who died aged 89 in 1987), and *Night Unto Night*, a 'cheerless nuthouse melodrama' (Halliwell) with 39-year-old Ronald Reagan, who 30 years later would become President of the United States. . .

157

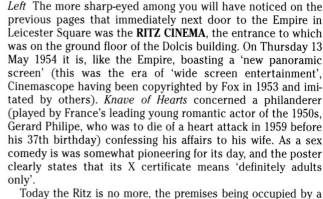

Left The more sharp-eyed among you will have noticed on the previous pages that immediately next door to the Empire in Leicester Square was the **RITZ CINEMA**, the entrance to which was on the ground floor of the Dolcis building. On Thursday 13 May 1954 it is, like the Empire, boasting a 'new panoramic screen' (this was the era of 'wide screen entertainment', Cinemascope having been copyrighted by Fox in 1953 and imitated by others). *Knave of Hearts* concerned a philanderer (played by France's leading young romantic actor of the 1950s, Gerard Philipe, who was to die of a heart attack in 1959 before his 37th birthday) confessing his affairs to his wife. As a sex comedy is was somewhat pioneering for its day, and the poster clearly states that its X certificate means 'definitely adults only'.

Today the Ritz is no more, the premises being occupied by a branch of Baskin Robbins, the American ice-cream company; the first floor of the Dolcis building is a restaurant, while the former Forte's restaurant is a branch of the Deep Pan Pizza Co, once again demonstrating the cosmopolitanism of modern London! *C. F. B. Penley, A. Mott collection/WA*

Below On the opposite (south) side of Leicester Square is the former **LEICESTER SQUARE THEATRE** of 1930, now the Odeon West End. Back in 1953 the cinema was advertising the European première of Disney's *Peter Pan*. Critics objected to Disney's interference with the plot (as he had also done with *Alice in Wonderland* two years earlier), and his use of the voice of 16-year-old American boy star Bobby Driscoll as Peter (he was another film actor who was to die young, in 1968 aged 31, in poverty and a drug addict). As a recent critic said, 'If you can view it without thinking of Disney messing [not the actual word used!] about with yet another children's classic and relax in the studio's last decent use of Technicolor, then you're in for a treat.' The supporting short, *Nature's Half Acre*, was one of Disney's celebrated live-action 'True-

Life Adventure' series, which won the Oscar as best two-reel short at the 1951 ceremony, hence the statuettes on the hoarding. Parked outside the cinema is a Hillman Minx convertible, and in the foreground a 'razor-edge' Triumph Renown.

Not only the Toys but also Walt Disney Pictures are back in town 43 years later! State-of-the-art animation in 1996 is represented by Disney's *Toy Story*. Having made the first full-length animated feature, *Snow White and the Seven Dwarfs*, in 1937, this was the first ever full-length computer-animated feature. As the *Empire* magazine reviewer commented, 'The result proves so breathtaking that two-dimensional cartoon fare will never seem the same again and offers further, glorious proof that movies aimed at junior cinemagoers are quite often miles better than those directed at their parents.'

Back in 1953 Leslie Nielson was about to make his first film. He made his name playing rugged cops or similar, until in *Airplane* (1980) and later *The Naked Gun* (1988) he revealed a great talent for straight-faced playing in zany comedies, although critics felt that *Spy Hard* was perhaps a spoof too far. . . *C. Mott, A. Mott collection/WA*

This page The **ODEON CINEMA, LEICESTER SQUARE** celebrated its 60th anniversary in 1997, its 'black and showily austere' frontage (Pevsner) having been built in 1937 on the site of the Alhambra theatre. From its opening in 1854 until its demolition in 1936, the Alhambra saw a varied succession of entertainment from circus and music hall to revue, ballet and opera. This very snowy view, taken by Mr Penley from the upper storeys of his Empire cinema in 1954, shows the film on release to be Norman Wisdom in *One Good Turn*. Londoner Wisdom left school at 14 and made his first stage appearance at Collins's Music Hall in Islington in 1946. This was his second film, but unlike the first, *Trouble in Store*, it was an 'unmitigated disaster' (Halliwell). However, that didn't stop Norman Wisdom going on to enjoy a long and successful career, being Britain's biggest comedy star until the mid-1960s. Note that his co-star is another stalwart entertainment veteran, Thora (now Dame Thora) Hird. Some parked cars, a motor coach, a taxi and a cabmen's bothy complete this very atmospheric scene.

For many years the Odeon has played host to important cinema events, including the Royal Film Performance. In March 1997 a particular kind of cinema nostalgia is on offer. Twenty years after its first release, *Star Wars* and the other films in the trilogy are back, digitally enhanced, for a new generation of movie-goers. Star Mark Hamill was only two years old when *One Good Turn* was made. . . Pedestrianisation has transformed this side of the Square, and the cabmen's shelter is a long-disappeared relic of the past. *C. F. B. Penley, A. Mott collection/WA*

INDEX